College Applications

& Essays

Susan D. Van Raalte

4TH EDITION

ARCO
THOMSON LEARNING™

Australia • Canada • Mexico • Singapore • Spain • United Kingdom • United States

ARCO

THOMSON LEARNING

An ARCO Book

ARCO is a registered trademark of Thomson Learning, Inc., and is used herein under license by Peterson's.

About Peterson's

Founded in 1966, Peterson's, a division of Thomson Learning, is the nation's largest and most respected provider of lifelong learning online resources, software, reference guides, and books. The Education Supersite^{SM} at petersons.com—the Web's most heavily traveled education resource—has searchable databases and interactive tools for contacting U.S.-accredited institutions and programs. CollegeQuest® (CollegeQuest.com) offers a complete solution for every step of the college decision-making process. GradAdvantage^{TM} (GradAdvantage.org), developed with Educational Testing Service, is the only electronic admissions service capable of sending official graduate test score reports with a candidate's online application. Peterson's serves more than 55 million education consumers annually.

Thomson Learning is among the world's leading providers of lifelong learning, serving the needs of individuals, learning institutions, and corporations with products and services for both traditional classrooms and for online learning. For more information about the products and services offered by Thomson Learning, please visit www.thomsonlearning.com. Headquartered in Stamford, Connecticut, with offices worldwide, Thomson Learning is part of The Thomson Corporation (www.thomson.com), a leading e-information and solutions company in the business, professional, and education marketplaces. The Corporation's common shares are listed on the Toronto and London stock exchanges.

For more information, contact Peterson's, 2000 Lenox Drive, Lawrenceville, NJ 08648; 800-338-3282; or find us on the World Wide Web at: www.petersons.com/about

Fourth Edition

COPYRIGHT © 2001 by Susan Drachman Van Raalte

Previous editions © 1997, 1993, 1990, 1995

Previously published as *College Applications Step by Step*.

ISBN 0-7689-0693-8

Printed in the United States of America

10 9 8 7 6 5 4 3 2 1   03 02 01

Contents

Acknowledgments

There are many people whom I wish to thank for their contributions to *College Applications and Essays*. Without their involvement and support, this book would not have been written.

- Thank you to the people of the Scarsdale Adult School, who gave me the chance to develop and teach a course on how to write college applications. The approach and content I used in *College Applications and Essays* are a direct result of the workshops I have conducted at the Scarsdale Adult School for the past fifteen years.

- Thank you to Bonnie Siverd, who urged me to turn my course into a book.

- Thank you to Linda Moser for helping me think through the logic of the book and for being such a good listener.

- Thank you to Suzanne Arkin, who believed in this project and brought it to the attention of ARCO.

- Thank you to Susan Diamond, George Ehrenhaft, and Michael Gibbs, who took time from their very full lives to read my drafts, offer suggestions, and provide support.

- Thank you to Mara Bonfeld, Stuart Malina, Andrew Van Raalte, Regina Raphael, Diana Dreyfus, Ben Golden, Evan Chalfin, and Michelle Shalit, who wrote such wonderful essays and allowed me to include them in my book.

- Thank you to my parents, Sally and Stanley Drachman, for their continued enthusiasm.

- Thank you to Steven Pass for his patience in imparting his knowledge of computers to me.

- Thank you to Zealie for his continued encouragement and support.

Chapter 1

Writing College Applications: What It's All About

So you want to go to college.

You've spent the past twelve years of your life preparing for it. You even know which schools you want to attend. Now all you have to do is apply.

Sounds simple, but it's not.

For many students, writing college applications can be sheer agony. Here's why:

- Often, you worry about finding something important to say. At the age of sixteen or seventeen, you look at yourself and ask: "What do I do? I go to school, play a little soccer. So what?" Nothing that you've achieved or experienced seems remarkable enough to impress an admissions committee.

- Once you have figured out what to say, you must next struggle with how to say it. It's hard enough to write routine expository essays describing three characteristics of someone like Huck Finn. Now, as you apply to college, you must write lucidly and persuasively about yourself.

- To make matters worse, the demands of a college application are unlike any task you've ever done before. The volume of paper generated and the number of steps involved can be overwhelming. You'll need to develop techniques to stay on top of the paperwork, learn the mechanics of responding to short-answer questions, and understand what a school is really looking for when it poses a question.

Handling Your Parents

Senior year stress is not restricted to seniors; parents can feel it too. Since they care about you, they want you to be happy, do well in college, and succeed in life. But more immediately, they want to make sure you don't "blow it" on your application.

When parents become anxious, their instinct is to jump in and try to make everything all right. As a result, they often nudge and ask questions. They want to know when you sent away for applications, what you're saying in your essays, who's writing your recommendations, and more. The problem is often cyclical. The less they know, the more they ask.

Since you'll probably work better without pressure from your parents, you'll want to break the cycle. You can do this by keeping your parents posted on your progress and by showing them that you take the application process seriously.

Let them know, for example, when applications come in and go out. Share your essay ideas without relinquishing control. Tell them about any administrative difficulties, such as a lost teacher recommendation and what you plan to do about it. And, of course, let them know about any good news.

For most parents, letting them in on your application activities—without letting them take over-can go a long way toward alleviating their anxiety and the pressure they place on you.

These problems are often compounded by the emotional stress that accompanies senior year. During this time, both you and your parents are in a state of transition. You're ready for college and a chance to be more independent. But in order to grow, you must give up some of the safety you have at home. Giving up the known for the unknown can make you very anxious.

At the same time, your parents may be wrestling with demons of their own. When you start applying to college, your parents know their years of being needed are numbered. Although most parents want their children to grow up, watching you prepare to leave home can be hard on them.

In spite of all these headaches, applications really do serve a positive purpose. Applications are not demonic devices cooked up by sadistic admissions officers to take all the fun out of senior year. Instead, applications can:

■ Help you reflect on who you are and what you want to accomplish in college and afterward, and

■ Provide one of the few opportunities to communicate directly with the admissions committee in your own words. In fact, your application may be your last chance to influence the admissions decision.

A Note to Parents

Because high school seniors are the ones who are going to college, the burden of completing their applications belongs to them. Family, friends, and counselors can pour out advice, telling applicants what to do. But the truth is, only the applicants can make the decisions and act on them.

As a parent, this truth can make you anxious. You wonder if your children will ever send away for applications, complete them properly, and get them in on time. And, you wonder, how can they possibly accomplish all this without YOU?

While your instinct may be to jump in and make everything all right, DON'T!

College Applications and Essays was developed to give students the help they need. In its pages, they will be coaxed and prodded by an objective professional through a step-by-step system designed to break down application writing into manageable pieces. They'll learn how to analyze their reader, analyze themselves, select a topic, and develop it well. They'll also learn how to get organized, get started, and stay on top of the paperwork.

Your children will benefit more from your support than from your interference. By encouraging them without prodding, by listening without judging, you can give your children the message that they're competent enough to handle their applications on their own.

This book is designed to help you make the most of this opportunity. In its pages, you will be coaxed and prodded through a step-by-step system designed to break down application writing into bite-sized pieces. You'll learn how to analyze your reader, analyze yourself, select a topic, and develop it well. You'll also learn how to get organized, get started, and stay on top of the paperwork.

A unique feature of this book is its participatory approach. Instead of merely describing techniques, this book will give you a chance to try them out. As you work through the following exercises, you will actually be writing your application. All you'll have to do when you reach the last page is put a stamp on the envelope and drop the application in the mailbox. Or, if you're applying electronically, you may only have to press the "send" button!

Here's a brief overview of each chapter:

■ Chapter 2: Getting Organized
Right away you'll get a sense of mastery as you learn how to get organized and stay on top of the paperwork. In this chapter you'll become familiar with the ten administrative steps involved in producing a complete application, and you'll develop a follow-up system to help you keep track of your work.

■ **Chapter 3: Understanding the Questions**

In this chapter you'll focus on the questions themselves and learn to assess how much writing you'll have to do by determining which essays can be reused in some variation.

■ **Chapter 4: Taking a Personal Inventory**

As you take an inventory of your feelings and experiences, you'll learn how to look for the facts and developments in your life that can form the basis for interesting essay answers. In addition, this chapter will show you how to handle the short-answer questions on your applications.

■ **Chapter 5: Selecting Your Topic and a Persuasive Approach**

In this chapter you'll learn how to analyze yourself and your reader to find the points you have in common. With this knowledge, you'll be better able to select a topic and a strategy that will help you project your best self on paper.

■ **Chapter 6: Crystalizing Your Ideas for Your Long and Short Essay Questions**

Having selected a topic and an approach that will show you off to advantage, you can begin to consolidate your thoughts. The exercises in this chapter will help you connect your thoughts, formulate the central idea for each of your essays, and outline your supporting ideas.

■ **Chapter 7: Structuring Your Essay for Busy Readers**

Because admissions officers are busy people, you'll want your essays to guide your readers easily from point to point. In this chapter you'll learn a couple of approaches to writing well-organized essays.

■ **Chapter 8: Beginnings and Endings Can Make a Difference**

This chapter throws a lifeline to students who can't find a catchy way to begin or bring their essays to a meaningful close. In a lesson that discusses and gives examples of several techniques, you'll learn how to begin and end your essays and select the approach best suited to your subject matter.

■ **Chapter 9: How to Keep Your Reader Reading**

It won't matter what you have to say if you turn your readers off with an offensive tone or a stodgy writing style. To help keep your reader reading, this chapter will show you how to identify and use an appropriate tone and will review some stylistic devices that can pump life into your essays.

■ **Chapter 10: Overcoming Fear of the Blank Page**
With a final plan for your essay in hand, you're ready to write. For those who have trouble getting started, this chapter gives you pointers that can help you write more efficiently and with greater confidence.

■ **Chapter 11: From Rough Draft to Finished Product**
In this chapter, you'll be introduced to the five stages of revision, and you'll be given a checklist to help identify your strengths and weaknesses.

■ **Chapter 12: Recycling Your Essays for Use on More Than One Application**
This chapter shows you how to adapt an essay so that it can be used to answer several different questions for several different applications.

■ **Chapter 13: Applying Electronically**
In this chapter you'll learn what kinds of electronic applications are available and how you can use them with ease.

Chapter 2

Getting Organized

Before you begin to worry about what to say and how to say it, it's a good idea to familiarize yourself with the administrative steps involved in producing a complete application. As you work through this chapter, be sure to follow the steps in the order they appear and to apply them to every application.

If you are applying electronically or if you plan to use computer-generated applications, be sure to read Chapter 13 for some important differences in these steps.

THE 10 STEPS TO WRITING AN APPLICATION

1. Set up a filing system.
2. Make copies of your blank applications.
3. Decide the order in which to work on your applications.
4. Distribute the appropriate parts of your application to the right people.
5. Arrange for your standardized test scores to be sent to your colleges.
6. Set up a follow-up system.
7. Write a rough draft, and revise it until it's the best you can make it. (This is obviously the hardest step!)
8. Transfer your answers onto the original application form.
9. Make copies of all your completed forms.
10. Send your application.

STEP 1: SET UP A FILING SYSTEM

To help you keep track of the materials each college sends you, you will need a 10x13 inch manilla envelope for each college to which you are applying. Be sure to get envelopes, not folders, because you can stuff envelopes with notes, rough drafts, view books, and correspondence, and none of it will fall out!

STEP 2: MAKE COPIES OF YOUR BLANK APPLICATIONS

It's easy to make mistakes on applications, especially if you are handwriting or typing a paper application. For example, you can misinterpret a question, write an answer in the wrong place, or misjudge the amount of space available. Any of these errors can negatively affect the admissions committee's attitude toward you, so you'll want to make sure you send in an application that's as close to perfect as possible.

To do this, make at least one copy of each blank application, and practice writing your answers on the copy first. Then, when you're satisfied that you've answered the questions correctly and that they'll fit in the space provided,* you can transfer your answers to the official application.

If you are typing your answers on line, you may need to abbreviate your responses to short answer questions, so your answers will fit into the limited space provided.* If you need more space for your essay, check to see if the application provides additional space for you to continue your response. If not, you may have to attach an extra page.

STEP 3: DECIDE THE ORDER IN WHICH TO WORK ON YOUR APPLICATIONS

When you apply to more than one college, you'll need to decide the order in which to work on your applications. In making your decisions, you should be guided by these two principles:

1. Meet Your Deadlines

You could have written the most fabulous essay or broken the curve of the SATs, but the schools may never know this if you don't get your completed application in on time. Colleges are very serious about their deadlines. As one university put it in a letter to students requesting application materials beyond the application deadline:

> You might want to consider carefully whether to submit a late application when so many other students have completed the process on schedule. Naturally, we feel a primary obligation to those candidates who have met our deadlines and whose applications are already completed for our evaluation. We will review their applications first and then proceed to review any late applications. Competition for admission will be extraordinarily keen for all candidates, especially for late applicants.

---

* Please see page 82 for a discussion on the length of your answers.

2. Determine Your Priorities

As a general rule, it's a good idea first to direct your energy and enthusiasm toward the schools you know you want to attend. Then, if there's time, you can work on the applications for schools that you're not quite as excited about.

Early Decision

- If you have a first-choice school, you might want to apply using the Early Decision option. This option enables you to declare that you'll definitely attend that school if you're accepted. In return for you pledge, which is binding and means you must attend that school and withdraw any applications to other schools, the college agrees to let you know of its decisions early, usually in December or January. Most schools offer an Early Decision 1 (ED1) plan for those students who have made up their minds by November, and some schools offer an additional plan, Early Decision 2 (ED2), for those students who make up their minds a month or two later. Here are some reasons why students might want to apply using the ED2 option:

  - You are rejected by your ED1 school, and you would like to try again with your second-choice school.

  - You are a fall athlete, and you need time to create a video and assemble a record of your sports accomplishments.

  - You couldn't decide between two favorite colleges, so you apply to one using ED1 and the other using ED2.

  - Please remember that if you're accepted by your ED1 school, you are obligated to attend that school, and you must withdraw all applications to other schools.

- If you're applying early decision, be sure to prepare your other applications so they're ready to go before you're notified of your early decision status. In this way, if you're deferred or rejected, you can avoid the panic of preparing several applications at the last minute, as well as the psychological letdown that can interfere with your motivation to work on them.

Rolling Admissions

- If you're applying to a college with a rolling admissions policy, try to get your application in as soon as possible, especially if this college is one of your first choices. Since colleges with rolling admissions policies fill up places in their classes as they receive applications, your chances for admission are better when more spaces are available. Of course, if you're not certain you want to go to this school, or you're taking your SATs again, you can put off this application for a while because there is usually no set deadline.

Keeping these principles in mind, fill in the chart on the next page. You may want to refer to it on a regular basis to make sure you complete all of your applications on time.

COLLEGE	EARLY DECISION DEADLINES ED1/ED2	REGULAR DEADLINE OR ROLLING ADMISSION	IF YOU DEFINITELY PLAN TO APPLY TO THIS SCHOOL PLEASE CHECK (✓)

STEP 4: DISTRIBUTE THE APPROPRIATE PARTS OF YOUR APPLICATION TO THE RIGHT PEOPLE

When you know which colleges you want to apply to, you should distribute the appropriate parts of your application to your counselor and teachers. By enabling them to work on their evaluations while you work on your application, you can reduce the time it takes to complete your file for admission. Of course, if you're applying for early decision, you'll want to get that application going first. (Please see box on page 10.)

Before you hand out these forms, however, you need to consider two important issues:

1. Waiving Your Rights to See Material in Your File

The Family Educational Rights and Privacy Act, also known as the Buckley Amendment, allows students to know what statistical and evaluative information is in their academic files. The Amendment was passed to protect students from incorrect and even slanderous statements that could in some way affect their future.

While the intent of the Amendment is noble and good, it unfortunately has some drawbacks. First, you can only see your file at the school where you officially matriculate. Second, you can have access only to materials in your permanent file. Since not all schools consider admissions materials to be part of your permanent record, you may not always be able to read what people have written about you. For these reasons, the Amendment does little to protect you during the application process.

In addition, many counselors and teachers, fearing legal reprisals for making truthful, if less than flattering, statements, have chosen to whitewash

Who Gets What

Your application consists of several forms. Some you fill out yourself. Others you give to your counselor and teachers.

You fill out:

- *The student application form consisting of short-answer questions (SAQs) and essays.*

- *If you're applying for financial aid, you must complete the FAFSA form (available on line or through your counselor) or the needs analysis form from either the College Scholarship Service or the American College Testing Program. Be sure to ask the college to send you financial aid information and forms when you initially request an application for admission.*

Your counselor fills out:

- *A secondary school report, which includes your class rank, a transcript of your courses and grades, and a general evaluation of your academic ability and personal integrity.*

- *A mid-year report, which reports the grades for first semester of the current school year.*

Your teachers fill out:

- *A recommendation form, which invites a teacher to describe your personal characteristics and academic abilities. Since your teachers often know you better than your counselor, this recommendation usually gives a more detailed analysis of your qualifications than the secondary school report.*

their comments. As a result, admissions officers give less weight to positive recommendations that the student has a right to see under the Buckley Amendment.

To overcome this problem, some colleges give students the option of waiving their right to see their admissions files by signing a statement that frequently appears on the teacher recommendation form and on the secondary school report form. Since teachers usually feel freer to give a more accurate picture of your abilities if you waive your right to see the recommendation, many authorities on college admissions advise students to sign these waivers.

2. Deciding Who Should Write Your Recommendations

Since the people you select to write your recommendations can make a difference in the way the admissions committee perceives you, it's important to choose teachers who know you, like you, and feel that they can do a good job for you.

Keep in mind that each college requests a certain number of recommendations, and that is precisely the number you should submit.

So if a college asks for two recommendations, don't send three; if a college asks for three recommendations, don't send two; and if a college asks for none, don't send any!

It's perfectly all right to size up your student-teacher relationship by directly asking the teacher if he or she could write a strong recommendation in support of your candidacy. If the teacher says no or if you sense any reluctance on the teacher's part, it's best to say something like "I'll understand if you're too busy." In this way, the teacher can decline gracefully, and you can feel free to ask someone else.

If you feel a teacher would be better able to write a strong recommendation if he or she knew more about your life outside the classroom, by all means try to arrange an appointment to discuss your activities, interests, and goals. Just be sure you approach the teacher gently and with tact. Nothing will turn off a teacher faster than a pushy student.

Consider teachers who can add insight or depth to your application. A teacher whom you've had for more than one course or with whom you've worked closely on a project can do this for you. It's also helpful to select someone who has taught you recently. Since colleges know students can change dramatically from their freshman to their senior year, the comments from an 11th-grade teacher may be more helpful than comments from a 9th-grade teacher. However, comments from a teacher who has watched you grow, having taught you in both grades 10 and 11, are very valuable.

If you have talents that you would like to highlight, select teachers who have firsthand knowledge of these abilities. If you write for the school newspaper, for instance, and you feel this experience enhances your candidacy, you can ask the teacher who serves as newspaper adviser to write a recommendation for you.

And if you pursue an interest outside of school, you can submit a supplemental letter from the adult most familiar with your work. This letter should contribute new information to your file but not take the place of a required school recommendation. Since admissions people may resent the extra reading, it's advisable to submit only one outside recommendation—and only if it will strengthen your application substantially. (Please see box on page 13.)

STEP 5: ARRANGE FOR YOUR STANDARDIZED TEST SCORES TO BE SENT TO YOUR COLLEGES.

Once you've given your counselor and teachers their forms to fill out, you should arrange for your standardized test scores (SAT, ACT Assessment, etc.) to be sent directly from the appropriate testing service to your selection of colleges. If you've taken the SAT, or Achievement Tests, you should contact the Educational Testing Service in Princeton, New Jersey. If the ACT Assessment is required, you should contact ACT, Inc. in Iowa City, Iowa. Your counselor can tell you how to get in touch with these services.

Depending on the service you use, you will be allowed to send your scores to either three or four schools when you register for the test. If you're applying to more schools, you can obtain additional score report forms from your counselor. These forms authorize the testing services to send your scores to additional colleges.

While photocopies of your test results may be acceptable on an interim basis at some colleges, keep in mind that an official copy of the results must be received by the college before you will be notified of an admission decision.

You can also reach your testing service of choice by going on line. For more information, please see Chapter 13.

STEP 6: SET UP A FOLLOW-UP SYSTEM.

Now that you've distributed all the parts of your application to the appropriate parties, you need to develop a system that will help you keep track of how everyone's doing. A good follow-up system is especially important since your application will not be reviewed by the admissions committee until it is complete.

The "Follow-Up" chart at the end of this chapter is designed to help you monitor your progress on your applications. To use this tool, simply follow these instructions:

1. For each college, tape a copy of the "Follow-Up" chart onto the outside of your manila envelope.

2. At the top of the chart, write in the name of the college, its mailing and e-mail address, the phone number of the school, the fax number, the Web site address, and the date the completed application is due.

3. In the column marked "date," write down when you took action on each step in the application process.

4. If, after you've completed the entire "date" column for a particular college, you have not received a notice from the admissions office telling you that your file is complete or that certain forms are missing, it's a good idea to call the admissions office directly to ensure it has received all your papers. Before you rush to the phone, however, be sure you've allowed enough time, usually four to six weeks, for your teachers and guidance counselor to complete and send in the forms and for the admissions office to receive and process them.

Once you know what's missing from your file, you can take action. If a test score is missing, you can contact the appropriate testing service. If a recommendation is missing, you can speak to the person responsible for writing it. It may be that the recommendation is, indeed, at the college but has yet to be processed.

Recommendation Etiquette

*T*he following memo, written by the chairman of the English department at a college-preparatory high school in the northeast, highlights the points you should keep in mind when you ask teachers to write recommendations.

TO: Seniors

FROM: The English Department

RE: College Recommendations

As you are aware, writing a college recommendation that presents an accurate and vivid portrait of a student is extremely demanding and time-consuming. The average length of the time required to do a good job ranges from one and a half to two hours for each letter. Teachers are not given time by the administration to compose letters of recommendation; they always take the time from their personal lives. We write the letters because we care about you and your future.

To help all of us, we request that you abide by the following procedures:

1. Please do not ask more than one member of the department to write a recommendation for you, since no college requires a recommendation from more than one English teacher.

2. It's best to ask your teachers early in the fall if they will write recommendations for you. In this way, you'll avoid being disappointed if your teachers turn you down because they already have more recommendation requests than they can handle.

3. Please request recommendations for only those schools to which you are definitely applying. If possible, wait until you've received the bulk of your applications before you approach us to write recommendations. In this way, teachers can better gauge the amount of work they have to do for you.

4. Make certain that you allow at least one month (not counting vacation time) for the teacher to meet the deadline for your school. It will help if you can supply the teacher with a list of your colleges and their deadlines.

5. Give the teacher a stamped envelope filled out with the address of the college admissions office and the return address of the teacher and high school for each school you are applying to.

6. Make certain that you have filled in your part of the application so that we do not have to find you to complete the information.

7. Remember that you are asking a teacher to do something for you. After a teacher has spent considerable time working on your behalf, you should take the trouble to tell that teacher, when the time comes, which school you finally selected.

Thanks very much for your cooperation.

If you've been courteous in this way to your teachers, you should feel confident that they'll be happy to write your recommendations. It's also a good idea to check back with your teachers in three or four weeks to ask them if they have any questions. If they do, you can provide answers. If not, your follow-up can gently remind them to get your recommendation out on time.

It's easy to feel disappointed or even betrayed when someone fails to write a recommendation for you. But as upset as you might be, resist the urge to make angry accusations. You should first consider that there might be a good reason. Perhaps a teacher is waiting for you to finish an assignment so the recommendation can reflect a fuller range of your academic achievements. Or perhaps the teacher has not forgotten you but is just swamped with other commitments.

Whatever the reason, the situation calls for the utmost of tact. No matter how angry you may feel, the reality is that you still need the teacher to write a recommendation—and a good one at that.

So instead of screaming at Miss Schulz: "You blockhead, my file is being held up because you didn't send in my recommendation!" you can simply say, "Somehow there was a mix-up, and ABC College has no record of receiving your recommendation. Do you think you could send off a copy?" By implying that Miss Schultz actually wrote the recommendation but the college misplaced it, you allow her to save face in the event she really did forget.

After you've taken action to correct any omissions in your file, you should receive notification that it is complete. If you do not, you might want to call the college again to make sure that everything is finally in order.

STEP 7: WRITE A ROUGH DRAFT, AND REVISE IT UNTIL IT'S THE BEST YOU CAN MAKE IT.

Now that you've taken care of all this administrative business, you're ready to write your applications. As a general rule, start with your short-answer questions and then move on to the more difficult part, the essay. It's usually a good idea to skim through your applications, writing out the essay questions on a piece of scratch paper. In this way, you can get a feel for the number and kinds of different essays you will be required to write.

Start by working on a rough draft that represents your first attempt to consolidate your thoughts. Several of the chapters in *College Applications and Essays* will help you with this initial effort and will guide you through the stages of revisions required to produce an interesting, thoughtful, and cohesive essay.

STEP 8: TRANSFER YOUR ANSWERS ONTO THE ORIGINAL APPLICATION FORM.

If you're applying using a paper application and you've polished your short-answer questions (SAQs) and essays into their final form, you're ready to transfer your answers onto the original application form. At this point, you may wonder if it's best to type or write. The answer is to do whichever produces the neatest results with the greatest ease.

If your handwriting is naturally neat, then writing may be a good option for you. If, on the other hand, you're pretty good with a typewriter, and you have easy access to one, you should consider typing. Under no circumstances should you feel pressured to type, especially if you're mistake-prone or if you type a word a minute.

Some students have successfully combined both methods in one application. They handwrite their SAQs so they can fit their answers neatly into the lines and boxes, and they type their essays for greatest legibility.

Whether you type or write, you'll want to steer clear of cross-outs, ink blots, food stains, or unusual colors of ink. If you do make a mistake, cover it neatly with a correction fluid such as White Out or Liquid Paper. (These fluids come in different colors and a variety of formulations to match different papers and cover different inks, such as typewriter ribbon or ballpoint pen.) Then type or write over the dried correction fluid.

Of course, if you're applying on line, you can make changes more easily. (Please see Chapter 13 for details on applying on line.)

STEP 9: MAKE COPIES OF ALL YOUR COMPLETED FORMS.

You'll want to make copies of your completed applications and keep them in your file. This way, you'll have a record of what you wrote, and you can act quickly in the event that a college does not receive or misplaces your application.

STEP 10: SEND YOUR APPLICATION.

Once you're satisfied that your application says what you want and represents your best work, and you've made a copy of it to keep on file, you're ready to send it. To make sure your application gets to its destination on time, if you are using the US Postal Service, you'll want to:

1. allow at least one week for the application to travel to the admissions office,

2. provide enough postage,

3. check the address to make sure it's correct and legible, and

4. include a return address in the event the post office must return your application to you.

The Common Application

The Common Application offers a single standardized application that is accepted by more than 200 colleges and universities. The beauty of the Common Application is that you—and your counselor—need to fill it out only once. Then, you simply make photocopies of the application, or print out copies if you're using your computer, and send them off to any of the participating colleges to which you wish to apply. To make the Common Application even more enticing, you usually have to write only one essay, which is accepted by all of the participating colleges.

Counselors love the Common Application. And as an increasing number of prestigious private colleges accept it, more and more students are taking advantage of it. But you should know that at the same time these participating colleges are moving toward simplicity and standardization in application procedures, several of them hold on to their individuality by accepting their own applications as well.

The move simultaneously toward standardization and individuality may seem contradictory until you realize that admissions officers have two primary concerns: one is to reach as many students as possible, and the other is to encourage those students to apply by simplifying the process. Clearly, the Common Application achieves both goals. What it doesn't do is allow each college to express its individuality. Because this is an important issue for private colleges, some of the colleges that use the Common Application will send you a supplementary form with additional questions (and frequently additional essays questions).

While more and more colleges are using the Common Application exclusively, some colleges offer students the option of applying with the school's own application or the Common Application. In this case, the question for you is: which application should you use? Admissions officers insist that there is no advantage to one application over the other. In fact, in order to be allowed to use the Common Application, a college must sign a statement saying that students will receive equal treatment regardless of whether they apply on the school's own form or on the Common Application.

One consideration that might help you decide which application to use is timing, especially if you are using a paper application and relying on the US Mail service. Obviously, if you are in a hurry, filling out the Common Application and writing one essay will get you into the application process quicker than completing several individual applications. If you are trying to meet an Early Decision deadline (usually November 1 or 15) at a college that requires you to fill out its own supplementary form in addition to the regular Common Application, waiting for the college to send you the supplement could really slow you down. In this case, you are probably better off using the college's own application because you will have the entire application in your hands at one time. However, if you're applying on line, the issue of timing becomes less of a factor since you can download both the Common Application and the college's supplement immediately.

The Common Application is available on disk through your counselor or the college itself, in both Windows and Mac versions. You can also find the Common Application on the Internet. When you receive a copy of the application, on paper, on disk, or on line, you will notice a cover page with a list of all the colleges accepting this application as well as a set of instructions. Be sure to read the information supplied by each college that tells you of its specific admissions requirements, such as its due date and whether or not you will need to fill out a supplementary application form.

FOLLOW-UP-CHART

College: _____   Phone: _____

Address: _____   Fax: _____

Application Due: _____   E-Mail: _____

Web: _____

ITEM	DATE	COLLEGE CONFIRMS RECEIPT OF:
Application materials requested		
Application materials received		
Student application form sent		
Check sent		
Financial Aid forms sent		
Needs-Analysis form (CSS or ACTs)		
College's own form		
Standardized Test Scores Request		
SAT (list dates taken)		
1.		
2.		
SAT II's (list subjects)		
1.		
2.		
3.		
Other: _____		
Secondary School Report		
Mid-Year School Report		
Letters of Recommendation		
1. _____ (name)		
2. _____ (name)		
3. _____ (name)		
Supplementary letter: _____ (name)		

Chapter 3

Understanding the Questions

Having familiarized yourself with the administrative steps in completing the application process, you are ready to start work on the applications themselves. In this chapter, you'll focus on the essay questions in order to assess the amount of writing you must do—that is, to determine how many essays can be reused, usually with some variation, for more than one college application—and, then, to make sure you know what you are really being asked to answer. Of course, if you're using the Common Application, you can reuse the same essay.

As you look through your applications, you may be surprised by the variety. Some colleges may require you to write several long and short essays, other colleges may ask for one major essay, and then other colleges may ask for no essay at all!

Many students take one look at the number of essay questions they are required to write and begin to panic. They assume that each question requires a fresh effort. Fortunately for you, colleges are interested in learning similar kinds of things about their applicants. As a result, you may find that certain questions are asked over and over again on your applications. The questions may not be the same word-for-word, but they may be similar enough for you to respond with a variation of an essay you have already written. You will learn techniques for reusing your essays in Chapter 12.

In the following chart, you can keep track of all the essay questions that appear on all your applications by following these instructions:

1. To begin, gather all your applications and arrange them in the order you listed them in step 3 of Chapter 2 (page 7).

2. Then, in the left-hand column of the following chart, write down the name of the college that appears first on your list.

3. In the right-hand column, begin to write down each essay question posed on that application. If you are given a choice of essays, write down all of the choices. This way, you won't make a decision on your options until you have had a chance to see if any other college is asking a similar question. Also, check to be sure you are writing the questions verbatim. If, by mistake, you change a word here or there, you could inadvertently change the entire meaning of the essay, resulting in an inappropriate answer.

4. After you have listed all of your questions for that application, write down the length requirements in the middle column for each essay. In some instances, the application will tell you exactly how long the essay should be. In other cases, you will need a ruler to measure how many inches of space you have been given for your response. Be sure to write down the number of inches, or pages, if that is the better measure, in the length column of the chart.

5. Once you have completed this process for all your applications, you are ready to assess the amount of writing you will have to do by cross-referencing the essay questions. In other words, you will want to note, in the margins of the chart, which essays are exactly the same and which ones are similar. You will also want to note which essays are the same but require a different treatment because of their length.

THE COMPLETE LIST OF ESSAY QUESTIONS

COLLEGE	LENGTH	ESSAY QUESTIONS

COLLEGE	LENGTH	ESSAY QUESTIONS

COLLEGE	LENGTH	ESSAY QUESTIONS

COLLEGE	LENGTH	ESSAY QUESTIONS

Having completed this chart, you are probably feeling some relief. Now you know that you can recycle some essays for use on other applications, resulting in less work for you. But, before your rejoice, it's important to make sure you understand what you're really being asked to answer and can differentiate among similar-sounding essay questions. The following analysis of some commonly asked essay questions will help you to do just that!

GENERAL ESSAY QUESTION

QUESTION	INTENT OF ESSAY QUESTIONS	SUGGESTIONS OR COMMENTS
A. "It is our aim to get to know you as well as possible through this application. With this in mind, please describe in detail some special interest, experience, or achievement or anything else you would like us to know about you. Essays on a personal, local, or national topic that is of particular concern to you are also welcome."	In essence, this question asks the student to "tell us something about yourself." Since the variety of suitable topics is so broad, the admissions committee is as interested in your choice of topic as it is in what you have to say about it.	Be sure to relate your topic to yourself. It's not enough to simply write about political unrest in South America or your involvement in the school play. In all cases, you'll need to show how your experiences have had an effect on you.
B. "Please ask and answer the one question that you wished we had asked."	Admissions committees want to learn about the "real" you. So, in order to elicit a genuine response from you, they encourage students to write about their own topics. In addition, this essay gives you some control in selecting your topic.	This question is a good one to choose, especially if you have already written a good essay in response to another question. You can recycle that essay here by posing a question that leads you to respond with the previously written essay.
C. "Please write about the topic of your choice."	As in question A, this essay choice requires you to narrow down a world of possibilities to a single topic.	Remember, what you choose to write about is as important as what you say and how you say it. This topic provides you with another opportunity to recycle a previously written essay.
D. "Please tell us any additional information that will give us a more thorough impression of you."	This question provides you with a place to tell the admissions committee about circumstances and events that you feel are important for them to know, such as: How a serious illness or divorce in the family affected your high school record.	Although you may feel that you don't have any "additional" information to tell, its to your advantage to use this space. If for nothing else, you can tell the admissions committee how much you would like to attend their college and play baseball, or the cello, or whatever, if you're admitted!

ESSAYS ON SPECIFIC TOPICS

ESSAY	INTENT OF ESSAY QUESTIONS	SUGGESTIONS OR COMMENTS
A. "Evaluate a significant experience, achievement, or risk that you have taken and its impact on you."	This question requires you to think and then write about something that either happened to you or that you made happen and then to consider how that occurrence might have affected you.	While this question limits students to a single significant event, you should feel free to follow this event over time to explain what you were like before, during, and after the occurrence.
B. "Discuss some issue of personal, local, national, or international concern and its importance to you."	This question not only tests your involvement in affairs outside of yourself, your school, and your family, but it also tests your knowledge and insights into these events.	If you select to answer this question, be sure that you really have an active interest in or a knowledge of these events. Otherwise your response could seem disingenuous.
C. "Indicate a person who has had a significant influence on you, and describe that influence."	This question assumes that students are shaped by their involvement with significant people in their lives. This requires you to think about the people who have had an impact on you and then to narrow down this group to one individual.	While the admissions committee is interested in learning about the person who influenced you, it is even more interested in the impact this person had on you. So, if you choose to write on this topic, remember to keep the essay primarily focused on you!
D. "Describe a character in fiction, an historical figure, or a creative work (as in art, music, science, etc.) that has had an influence on you, and explain that influence."	This question assumes you are affected by your academic, intellectual, and cultural experiences. This question requires that you evaluate these learning experiences in terms of how they might have changed your thinking, outlook, or interests.	Since some of the people reading your essay may not be familiar with the character or creative work you have chosen, be sure to give them some background information. But, mostly, keep the focus on you!

ESSAY	INTENT OF ESSAY QUESTIONS	SUGGESTIONS OR COMMENTS
E. "In brief, why do you believe this college is a good match for your academic and personal goals?"	The admissions committee is sincerely interested in your evaluation of how well matched you are with its college. With so many students applying to its school, the committee wants to select those students who can make a contribution to campus life and who are likely to accept it's offer for admission.	Before you answer this question, take the time to read the viewbooks and any other literature you may have about the college in order to find areas of interest that you and the college share. In your answer, be sure to specifically state the names of programs, courses, and activities you would like to pursue at that school.
F. "Which extracurricular activity has been especially important? Explain."	This question asks you to select one extracurricular activity and expand upon it.	In answering this question, avoid rehashing your awards, since you will have documented them elsewhere on the application. Instead, you should focus on why you like being involved in this activity and how you have evolved as a result of your involvement.

Taking a Personal Inventory

When you begin to work on your college applications, it's always a good idea to start with the short-answer questions (SAQs). Once they're completed, you'll feel as if you've made some real progress, and your responses can trigger ideas for your essays as well.

The Personal Inventory, beginning on page 29, is the tool that can help you respond clearly and appropriately to the SAQs and get your creative juices flowing. It is made up of several questions. The ones preceded by a bullet (•) can be found on most applications. The other questions—mainly the open-ended ones—are included to help you probe your attitudes and experiences for good essay ideas.

As you work on your SAQs and think about your essays, please keep in mind these important principles:

- **BE HONEST:** Simply stated, lying can provide automatic grounds for rejection. No matter how confident you are that you won't get caught, never fudge the facts on an application.

- **BE ACCURATE:** Nobody's perfect, but strive for perfection on your application. Unfortunately, your reader may interpret your mistakes, no matter how innocent, to be a sign of laziness, indifference, stupidity, or even dishonesty. So, be sure to check your grammar, spelling, and facts.

- **BE CONSISTENT:** While there is no one best way to present information for your SAQs, your reader will be looking for consistency in your approach. So, for example, if you spell out numbers at the beginning of your application, don't switch to numerals halfway through. Your consistency will make your application easier to read and give your reader the impression that you have really thought about your answers.

- ■ **BE COMMUNICATIVE:** Applications are standardized forms designed to get the most information from most students. On occasion, however, applicants may need to tailor a question or to submit additional information in order to give a complete picture of their qualifications.

  If you want to explain special circumstances affecting your application to the admissions committee, don't be apologetic or frightened. Simply put an asterisk or footnote next to the issue in question and explain the situation at the bottom of the page or where there is room. In extreme cases, such as when an illness or death in the family affects your grades, you could even write a separate letter. Frequently, colleges will provide space on the application for you to inform them of these circumstances. Just be sure you don't tell more than they need or want to know, or draw unnecessary attention to negative points.

With these principles planted firmly in your mind, you're ready to proceed to the Personal Inventory.

THE PERSONAL INVENTORY

The left-hand column of this chart asks many of the questions you'll find on your applications, as well as others that will help you start focusing your ideas for your essays. Fill in this column in order to have the answers available for reference as you complete your actual applications. The right-hand column provides suggestions and comments to help you fill out your SAQs correctly and get your thoughts together for writing the essays.

Let's start with some easy questions. Chances are, you can answer these without thinking. All the same, it's a good idea to get into the habit of writing your answers on a master sheet. In this way, you will always have the answers to application questions in one place where you can easily look them up.

VITAL STATISTICS

- Full Legal Name: _____

- Social Security Number: _____

- Date of Birth: _____
  Month, Day, Year

- Birthplace: _____
  City, County, Country

- Your Address:

  - Permanent: _____
    Street Address

  _____
  City/State Zip

  - Mailing: _____
    Street Address

  _____
  City/State Zip

- School Address: _____
  Official Name

  _____
  Street Address

  _____
  City/State Zip

- High School College
  Board/ACT Number: _____

Whenever you write your name, always use the same form. In this way, you'll save the admissions committee the trouble of figuring out if the "Billy Jones" on the application is the same person as the "William G. Jones" on the teacher recommendation form.

If your permanent address is different from your mailing address, be sure to include both.

When you refer to your high school, be sure to use its official name. Admissions people may not know that "The Ole Steamboat" (as you may fondly call it) is really the nickname for the Robert Fulton High School.

Your counselor can give you your College Board or ACT number.

FAMILY LIFE

- A. Name of

    Mother: _____
    Maiden Name

    Father: _____

- B. Occupation (describe briefly)

    Mother: _____

    _____

    Father: _____

    _____

- C. Education (Name of institution attended, when, and degree earned)

    Mother _____

    Father _____

- D. Brothers and Sisters (include names, ages, schools attended, degree and date earned)

    1. _____

    2. _____

    3. _____

    4. _____

Some of these questions require a little research. For example, you may need to ask Mom for a brief description of her job or Dad what year he graduated from college.

Although these questions may seem routine, your answers can give admissions officers more information than meets the eye. For example, they can learn something about your life at home: whether both your parents work, if you grew up in a blue collar or a white collar environment, or if your parents (or brothers and sisters) are alumni of the school. (We'll talk more about this situation later on, in chapter 5.)

Family-related issues can make wonderful essay topics. Here are some questions to start you thinking about your family life and how it has shaped you. These questions won't show up on a real, live application, but they can trigger some terrific ideas to develop in your personal essay.

List family experiences that have had an effect on you:

To answer this question, you need to think about how your family has helped to shape you into the person you are today. Please don't worry if your experiences don't seem to be earthshaking—very often, it's everyday living that can be most influential (and most interesting to an admissions office).

How have these experiences helped you to grow?

Some of the family situations you could list include:

—being an only child or one of many
—having a mother who has recently gone to work
—moving from town to town
—participating in a family activity or tradition such as an annual trip or an ethnic holiday celebration.

Which of your parents' traits would you most like to emulate?

Mother:

Here's another way to help you identify the kind of person you are. Thinking about your parents and their character traits can help you identify some of your values and where they came from. You might realize, for example, that your interest in social work originates from your mother's concern for the welfare of others. If this exercise should trigger an idea (or a piece of an idea) for your essay, be careful to focus your discussion primarily on *you,* not on your parents.

Father:

Which traits would you least like to emulate?

Mother:

Father:

ACADEMICS

- On the chart below, list all secondary schools you have attended from grades 9–12, starting with the school you are now attending.

This question shows up regularly on college applications. Some schools will provide you with a chart; others will simply leave a blank space. If the latter is the case, you may want to borrow the format below to help you organize and present your information clearly. In fact, all of the charts in the Personal Inventory are designed for this purpose.

NAME OF SCHOOL	LOCATION (CITY AND STATE)	DATES ATTENDED MONTH/YEAR

- Date of high school graduation:

_____
Month/Year

Your responses to the questions on this page may start you thinking about your education and its effect on you. If, for example, you attended more than one school or if you switched from public to private school, you might be able to draw some conclusions about yourself by comparing these educational experiences. If you stayed in one place, you might want to consider the advantages or disadvantages of this consistency.

- Type of high school (please check):

  Public ☐
  Private ☐
  Parochial ☐

- List the college board examinations you will have taken by February of your senior year.

Colleges frequently ask students to report their test scores on their applications. Since it's easy to forget dates and scores, write them down here so you'll have them all in one place for future reference.

TEST	DATES (MONTH/YEAR	SCORE (IF AVAILABLE)
SAT I	1.	
	2.	
ACT Assessment	1.	
	2.	
SAT II (list subjects)		
1.		
2.		
3.		

▪ Now let's take a look at what you studied in high school. For each year and subject, please fill in the course titles:

When this information is asked for on an application, it can help admissions people interpret the cryptic abbreviations that frequently show up on your official transcript. From a more personal point of view, this chart gives you the perfect opportunity to review your academic history.

	9th GRADE	10th GRADE	11th GRADE	12th GRADE
ENGLISH				
LANGUAGE				
SOCIAL STUDIES				
MATH				
SCIENCE				
P.E.				
ELECTIVES				
OTHER				

How many courses did you take in the humanities (English, Language, Social Studies, Arts, etc.)? _____

How many, if any, were:

  Honors _____ Accelerated _____

  Advanced Placement _____

How many courses did you take in Math and Science? _____

How many, if any, were:

  Honors _____ Accelerated _____

  Advanced Placement _____

Think about the courses you have taken and identify the topics, projects, or reports you found to be:

Satisfying

Dissatisfying

As you answer these questions, look for trends that can give you clues about your interests and abilities.

Okay, let's probe a little deeper.

In the chart above you identified your areas of general interest and expertise. Here you can focus on the specific subjects, teaching methods, and learning environments you particularly enjoyed (or disliked). Your answers can provide some substance for your personal essay as well as help you decide which courses, programs, and learning environments are best suited to you.

If you're having trouble answering this question, you can think about a particular session that was wonderful—or terrible. Try to identify what made the difference: subject matter? teaching style? student interaction? teaching materials? or in-class activities?

- Many colleges would like to know about the non-credit programs you may have participated in, such as: summer music programs, sports camps, language, art or travel-study programs.

In the chart below, please list them.

OFFICIAL NAME OF PROGRAM	LOCATION (CITY, STATE, OR FOREIGN COUNTRY)	DATES ATTENDED MONTH/YEAR

Why did you participate in these programs?

You might be tempted to simply say, "I thought this program would be fun" or "I had nothing else to do." But clearly that is not enough. Instead, you need to put your finger on what specifically appealed to you, such as: developing a special interest, exploring a new field, or being on your own away from home.

Did these programs influence you in any way?

When you answer this question, think about what you learned or how you changed as a result of the program.

By now, you may begin to see a pattern emerge from your interests, attitudes, and experiences. The charts and questions on the remaining pages of the "Personal Inventory" may provide other ideas that you can develop in your essays.

EXTRACURRICULAR ACTIVITIES

- On the chart on page 35, you can tell an admissions committee how you spend some of your time when you are not in class.

You may have many or few items to list here, depending on the amount of time you have available after school to participate in extracurricular activities.

As you fill in the chart, try to list all activities that come to mind. Later, after you have had a chance to look it over, you can prune and reorganize the list to emphasize the activities that make a positive statement about you. Be sure to include the following activities:

Extracurricular: art, clubs, dance, drama, music, publications, sports, etc.

Community: Fund raisers, political action groups, social services, etc.

Religious: Youth group, choir, etc.

Family Activities: Trips, projects, etc.

The example on the chart indicates that this student worked on the school newspaper for two years. In 10th grade, she spent seven hours per week writing about sports. Then in 11th grade, she was promoted to Sports Editor and her involvement and time commitment doubled.

ACTIVITY	GRADE LEVEL OR YEAR OF PARTICIPATION				APPROXIMATE NUMBER OF HOURS SPENT PER WEEK	POSITIONS HELD OR HONORS WON	DO YOU PLAN TO PARTICIPATE IN COLLEGE?
	9	10	11	12			
school newspaper 'The Red and the White'		✔	✔		7, 14	sports writer, sports editor	yes

Which activities have you consistently participated in (for at least two consecutive years)?

The way you spend your time outside of the classroom can tell you something about yourself. Sometimes these insights can generate ideas for an essay.

What originally attracted you to these activities?

As you think about why you joined an activity and chose to continue with it, look for trends or similarities. Sometimes there are links between different types of activities. For example, you may have joined the band and the soccer team because you like to contribute to a group effort.

What are the newest activities?

In the past year or so, you may have taken up a new activity. Think about why you decided to participate now (not earlier or later).

What made you try them?

Perhaps your new involvement can point to a change in your outlook or personal circumstances. For example, a new friend may have influenced you or a move to a new school might have given you a chance to try activities not offered at your previous school.

Now that you have thought through your reasons for joining activities, you can be more selective about the ones you want to show to a college. Contrary to popular opinion, a list with everything on it does not prove your diversity. More than likely, it can make you look like a dabbler.

Since colleges are impressed with students who seem to have a sense of direction, cross out any activities you joined for:

■ superficial reasons (such as the club you joined so that you could meet the school's heart throb), or
■ a very short time (such as a sport that you played for less than a season), unless the activity, like a model UN, is scheduled to meet for a discrete period of time.

Your activities should suggest your:

■ genuine and sustained interest,
■ ability, and/or
■ personal growth

Once you've assembled the items for your list, you need to arrange them logically. For example, you could organize your activities into:

■ broad categories, such as school-related/non-school-related, or
■ more specific categories, such as sports, publications, and community work.

Whatever you decide, your format should showcase your abilities and make sense to your reader.
Now, on the blank chart, please copy all your revisions.

ACTIVITY	GRADE LEVEL OR YEAR OF PARTICIPATION				APPROXIMATE NUMBER OF HOURS SPENT PER WEEK	POSITIONS HELD OR HONORS WON	DO YOU PLAN TO PARTICIPATE IN COLLEGE?
	9	10	11	12			

As you fill in this chart, think about the relative importance of these activities to you. One way to determine your priorities is to imagine that you have time for only two or three activities. The ones that you would want to continue doing under these circumstances are probably the most significant to you. In analyzing which activities are the most valuable to you and why, you may come up with an interesting idea for an essay.

HONORS

- Colleges are always interested in learning about any honors you may have received. In the following chart, list the honors you earned for scholastic, extracurricular, or community achievements.

DO NOT PANIC if you have nothing to put here. Relatively few people can claim an honor (that's what makes honors so special). In most cases, however, students can make up the weakness in this area with strengths in work experience and extracurricular activities.

HONOR	CRITERIA

As you name the honor, be sure to explain what you did to earn it. For example, if you were selected for membership in the school honor society, you should jot down that you needed to: maintain a high GPA, receive strong recommendations from the faculty, and participate in several extracurricular activities.

Like the other charts in the Personal Inventory, this one can provide a model to help you arrange similar information on your application.

WORK EXPERIENCE

Here's your chance to show the admissions committee the record of your work experience. Some of you may have a lot to show here. Others who have spent most of their time in extracurricular activities may have much less.

- On the chart below, list the jobs you have held, arranging them in chronological order, starting with the most recent. If you are lacking other work experiences, volunteer work can go on this page as well. Just make sure you don't double list these items on the extracurricular chart.

Here are some tips on filling in this chart:

Type of work:

list the kind of work, such as nurse's aid, newspaper reporter.

Volunteer/paid:

check the category that applies.

Employer:

list the company or organization, such as, Burger King or New York Hospital—not Mr. Joe Schmidt, unless he is a private practitioner.

Dates:

Include the month and year for the starting and terminating dates. For example: 6/01–8/01.

TYPE OF WORK	VOLUNTEER/PAID		EMPLOYER	DATES	HRS/ WEEK

Think about the jobs you have held and identify the aspects of your work experiences that you found to be:

The chart on page 39, like the ones listing your courses and your extracurricular activities, can reveal a great deal about your areas of interest and expertise.

Satisfying:

Now you can focus on the specific activities, work environments, and interactions you particularly enjoyed—or disliked. Your answers can provide some substance for your personal essay as well as help you decide which job situations are best suited to you.

Dissatisfying:

If you're having trouble answering this question, think about an aspect of the job that was terrific—or horrible. Pehaps you loved (or hated) the repetition of crunching out numbers on your calculator for weeks at a time. Or perhaps you loved (or hated) working in an office where so much was happening that you were never bored and never had a moment of peace.

COLLEGE AND CAREER PLANS

- Please state your intended college major:

The questions concerning your academic experiences, special programs, and extracurricular or work activities may have triggered some thoughts about your future.

- Please explain your career or professional plans:

While colleges are interested in your academic and career plans, they don't expect you to know exactly what you want to do or stick with this course of action forever. So, if you can't put down a specific interest, you can narrow the field down to a few. In this way, you can show the admissions committee that you have a sense of where you're going without committing yourself to a particular destination.

When you respond to questions about your career or major on your application, be sure your answers are compatible with your abilities. Don't, for example, say that you want to write the great American novel if your grades in English are mediocre or poor.

Congratulations! You have just finished one of the most difficult steps in writing your application: finding something to say. Based on what you have discovered about yourself, please use the space below to write down three possible topics you could develop into a personal essay. You will be using these answers for the exercises in Chapter 6.

1. _____

2. _____

3. _____

With this done, you're almost ready to focus exclusively on writing your short and long essays. But first, take some time to fill in the short-answer questions (SAQ's) for each application, making sure that you practice on a copy of your application before you transfer your answers to the original.

Chapter 5

Selecting Your Topic and a Persuasive Approach

Wh
hen you write your college applications, and more specifically the personal essays, your number-one goal is to make the reader want you enough to admit you. To increase your chances of getting this response, you'll need to find out what makes your reader "tick" and identify the assumptions and experiences you share.

This concept, called audience analysis, should influence all phases of your writing, including topic selection, idea development, word choice, and style. So when you are gathering your thoughts, the question is not just, "What ideas can I find that are relevant to my topic?" but also "What do I know about my reader's experiences and ways of seeing things that I can use to get him or her to relate to my topic?" Similarly, when you're organizing your thoughts, the question is not just, "What order makes the most sense?" but also "What order will make the most sense to my reader?"

You'll probably be relieved to learn that to "know thy reader" doesn't mean you'll have to find out the personal feelings of each member on the admissions committee. Rather, it means you'll want to understand how admissions officers as a group and in their professional capacity think and feel.

Since a school without students has no reason to exist, the work of the admissions committee is essential to the health of any college. Admissions officers understand the importance of their job, and they take it seriously. They work long hours searching for the students who are best suited and show a genuine desire to attend their school.

To find these students, admissions people are willing to sift through piles and piles of paper, frequently reading as many as fifty complete applications a day. As they read your transcripts, secondary school reports, recommendations, and essays, admissions people are looking to see if you can handle the academic workload and make a positive contribution to college life.

This analysis of your audience can give you clues about how to present yourself on paper. To get a favorable reaction from admissions people, your application should demonstrate:

- a serious intent to pursue a college-level education.

- a genuine desire to attend the particular college.

- a match between your interests and abilities and what the school needs and has to offer.

- an ability to think clearly, logically, and creatively.

- an ability to write engaging, thoughtful essays that keep your reader's attention and differentiate you from the pack.

In this chapter, we'll begin the essay-writing process by applying this reader-oriented approach to the selection and development of your topic. To help you with these tasks, you'll need to pay special attention to the two exercises that make up the bulk of this chapter:

Exercise 1

   Matching what a *college* wants with what you have to offer,

   and

Exercise 2

   Matching what *you* want with what a college has to offer.

MATCHING WHAT A COLLEGE WANTS WITH WHAT YOU HAVE TO OFFER

Although it's impossible to predict exactly what a particular college is looking for in its applicants, one can say in general that colleges are intent in admitting a mix of students who can individually contribute to the college experience. In other words, colleges are looking for individuals with strengths in different areas, academic or extracurricular, so that collectively they make up a well-rounded class. One highly competitive college refers to this process as "creating the brightest mosaic" from the applicants who shine the brightest in terms of their potential contribution to the college community. Alone, each student is only a shiny stone; collectively, all the students create a brilliant masterpiece.

In the exercise beginning on the next page, you'll learn to identify the categories in which you shine and the corresponding strategies that can help you convey your attributes to the admissions committee.

Be sure to read all the categories; don't just stop with the first one that fits you. If you're lucky enough to have two or more categories apply to you, then you can diversify your approach, using the strategy that works best for each college.

Also, don't be surprised if you find yourself flipping back to your Personal Inventory. The facts and ideas you collected there will provide the basis for any approach you choose to take.

Directions: For each category on the following pages, read the characteristics and check the ones that apply to you. Then read the comments in the strategy column, and think about ways you can approach your topic to create a positive response in your reader.

THE BRAIN*

CHARACTERISTICS		STRATEGY

You fit this category if you can claim most of these intellectual achievements.

Please ✓ the characteristics that apply to you:

Board scores in the 700s ☐

Several AP courses with test scores of 4 or 5 ☐

Top grades in difficult courses ☐

A very high GPA ☐

A genuine interest in learning as demonstrated by some independent academic project (such as ongoing research in a laboratory) ☐

If you fall into this category, your school record will make this point loud and clear. While most colleges are truly impressed with your brains, they will also want to know if there is more to you than your board scores and GPA reveal. This is particularly true if you are applying to the most competitive schools, where hundreds of other applicants are likely to be as academically brilliant as you.

You can demonstrate that you are not just another pretty transcript by:

1. showing a completely different side of you.

   ■ In this case, look in your Personal Inventory for the nonacademic experiences, interests, and values that make you the person you are.

or

2. discussing an aspect of your field of expertise that especially interests you (such as the treatment of women in Jane Austen's novels or the importance of a new laboratory technique). More specifically you can talk about

   ■ how your interest evolved and how you plan to pursue it in the future.
   ■ the emotional and intellectual challenge of working on a related project.

---

* The categories on this and the following pages have been suggested by Richard Moll in his book, Playing The Private College Admissions Game (New York: Penguin Books, 1986).

SPECIAL TALENT CATEGORY

CHARACTERISTICS

You fit this category if

- you have a special ability in one of the following

  AND

- you are willing to rely on this talent as your primary qualification for admission. (If you're not prepared to make this commitment, please see the All-American Kid category.)

Please ✓ the talent that applies to you:

Athletics ☐

    sport(s): _____

    _____

    position(s): _____

    _____

Music
    Instrument ☐
    Voice ☐
    Composition ☐
    Other ☐

Theater ☐

Dance ☐

Writing/Journalism ☐

Art/Photography ☐

Other ☐

STRATEGY

Before you choose to draw attention to your special interest, be sure the school wants what you have to offer. Your finesse with a lacrosse stick, for example, will buy you nothing if you're applying to a college with no lacrosse team. Similarly, a college may have an orchestra but no need for cellists this year.

When you write about your talent, you'll want to show your strengths without restating the obvious.

This means that, instead of restating the facts about the special lessons you take or the awards you won, all of which should be clear from your SAQs, try to give the reader some insight into your passion.

For example, you can discuss

- what appeals to you about playing football, the flute, or whatever.

- what you've learned about yourself as you've pursued your talent.

- how you have faced challenges and disappointments.

- how you plan to incorporate your talent into your life in college and beyond.

In some instances, you may be able to demonstrate your talent firsthand. For example, you may want to send slides of your artwork or a taped recording of your musical or singing ability. A trusted teacher in your area of special talent can help you prepare your demonstration.

THE ALL-AMERICAN KID CATEGORY

CHARACTERISTICS

Please ✓ the characteristics that apply to you:

You fit this category if two or more of the following apply to you:

- You are bright but not a "Brain."* (See page 45) ☐

- You have well-developed talents but are not a "Special Talent."* (See page 46) ☐

- You've held offices or participated in student government or school organizations such as clubs. ☐

- You've held an editorship or participated in the school yearbook or newspaper. ☐

- You are a well-intentioned, nice person. ☐

- You generate ideas and enthusiasm. ☐

- You follow through on projects and get things done. ☐

- You get others to get things done. ☐

- You want to contribute to

  - the college community by participating in extracurricular activities. ☐

  - the outside community by devoting time to social services, political causes, or business activities. ☐

- Other: _____ ☐

STRATEGY

Since so many applicants can fit this category, it is especially important for you to find a way to differentiate yourself from the masses and highlight your assets.

The key here is to get your reader to know and like you. In your discussion,

- focus on what your experiences mean to you and how you've grown.

- tie in relevant aspects of your personal or family life (without unloading embarrassing or intimate details on your reader).

If you can demonstrate unusual maturity, sensitivity, and direction in your essay, you'll be ahead of the game.

And, as we discussed in other categories, you'll want to show your strengths in new ways without restating the obvious.

* These statements do not exclude the "Brain" or "Special Talent" applicant from this category. In most cases, a "Brain" or an applicant fitting any of the other categories could demonstrate a number of the characteristics listed here.

The applicant who fits the All-American Kid category as well as any of the others has the option of deciding among strategies.

MINORITY CATEGORY

CHARACTERISTICS

You fit this category if you are

Please ✓ the characteristics that apply to you:

- a black African American, an American Indian or Alaskan Native, an Asian American, a Hispanic or Latino, or a member of any other federally recognized minority. ☐

  OR

- handicapped—and able to pursue a college education in spite of the difficulties imposed by your handicap. ☐

  OR

- a member of any special group that the college is trying to attract. For example:

  - an urban college may want to attract students from rural areas. ☐

  - an all-male school, going coed for the first time, will want to seek female students. ☐

  - a well-endowed private college may want to attract a few outstanding students from "disadvantaged" backgrounds. ☐

- Other: _____ ☐

STRATEGY

While you don't want to hide your minority status, avoid calling direct attention to it or implying in any way that you should be accepted simply because you're a minority.

- This means, do not say something like, "I'm an American Indian; I can fill your minority quota!"

Instead, think about the way your minority status has shaped your personality and outlook, and subtly weave this point of view into your writing. For example, you might want to talk about a problem you have faced as an African American in a largely white school and how you have overcome it or describe an attitude of the culture you come from and how it has helped you accomplish certain goals. But don't lay it on too thick; you have to demonstrate that you're special as an individual, not just special because you happen to belong to a minority group.

THE ALUMNI CHILD

CHARACTERISTICS	STRATEGY

CHARACTERISTICS

Please ✓ the characteristics that apply to you:

You fit this category if:

Either (or both) of these relatives attended the school you're applying to:

Mother ☐
Father ☐

STRATEGY

The only alumni that really count with the admissions committee are parents. The fact that your aunt graduated in 1960 or that your sister is currently attending may be a point of interest. But in general, these relationships do not carry much weight in the admissions process. If several generations of your immediate family attended the school, however (for example, Dad, Granddad, and Great-granddad), that's best of all.

While a close alumni relationship can give you an edge over other applicants, you must demonstrate to the admissions committee that you can contribute to the school in your own right.

This means

- do not rely on your alumni ties to get you into college.

- do not write an essay that focuses on the joy of being a legacy.

Rather, go back to your Personal Inventory and look for the abilities, qualities, and achievements that would make you an asset to the college community. Consider yourself as belonging to at least one other category in addition to Alumni Child, and proceed accordingly.

These five categories should have started you thinking about a topic and an approach that can help you present yourself persuasively on paper. Next, you'll want to match what *you* want in a school with what a school has to offer.

MATCHING WHAT YOU WANT WITH WHAT A COLLEGE HAS TO OFFER

Although this book assumes you know which colleges you want to apply to, this next step can make sure you screen out the colleges that don't really make sense for you. After all, there's no good reason to waste your time and energy writing applications for schools that you don't want to attend.

But more to the point, your research from the following exercise can put you in a better position to show your reader, the admissions committee, why you and the college are well suited. In fact, once you know this information, answering a question like, "Why do you think our school is a good match for you?" will be easy for you, whether it shows up on the application or during an interview. In addition, admissions officers are usually impressed with students who have taken the time to learn about their school, and they'll be favorably impressed if you can demonstrate that you'll be both happy and productive there.

Evaluating the match between what you want and what the college offers can also save you from making stupid or embarrassing statements, such as saying, "I'm happiest when I'm acting" to a school with no drama department or "I work best when I'm under pressure" to a school with a pass-fail grading system designed to encourage a relaxed learning environment. Admissions officers often interpret these statements to mean that you don't care enough about the school to find out what it offers or simply that you won't fit in.

This exercise will help you analyze the fit between you and the colleges you're considering. Since this is an important step, you'll want to complete this exercise for each college.

Before you begin, gather any catalogs and viewbooks published by each college and the notes you may have taken during your discussions with admissions officers, students, guidance counselors, and other knowledgeable people. From these sources, you can piece together an accurate picture of each school.

Try to answer each question as thoroughly as you can, even if it takes a lot of time. And don't let pressure from your parents, friends, or guidance counselors cloud your ability to honestly evaluate the schools. You may ultimately decide that these people are right-or wrong-but your decision should be made because you have intelligently analyzed how well each school will meet your needs.

Directions: Working across the page, (1) write in the facts about each characteristic, (2) read the comments in the next column and think about them, and (3) write in your personal reaction. On the last page, summarize your overall reaction and make your final decision to apply or not to apply.

School: _____

CHARACTERISTICS	COMMENTS	YOUR FEELINGS ABOUT EACH CHARACTERISTIC
NOTE: Many of these facts can be found in viewbooks, catalogs, and college guides.	The information presented in this column can help you evaluate each characteristic.	*In this column, put down whether you like or dislike this characteristic and how important it is to you. If you can, explain why you feel this way.*
School Philosophy (please summarize):	The school philosophy is important to know because it can give you clues to the school's personality and how the school likes to perceive itself. You can usually find a statement of the school philosophy in the first few pages of the viewbook or in the college catalog.	

Size
  Number of students attending:
  _____ full-time
  _____ part-time
  _____ graduate students
	Some questions to consider:
	
	■ Will a small school provide enough stimulation for your continued growth over four years?
	
	■ Are the elaborate facilities usually associated with larger universities (e.g., gymnasium, laboratory) essential to your studies?
	
	Keep in mind that a small school may seem to offer as many courses and other opportunities as a large school, to judge from the catalog, but in fact some of these courses and activities may rarely materialize because there aren't enough students to fill them. On the other hand, a small school may offer a more intimate and supportive environment.	

School: _____

CHARACTERISTICS	COMMENTS	YOUR FEELINGS ABOUT EACH CHARACTERISTIC
Location (please ✓): ☐ Northeast ☐ Southeast ☐ Midwest ☐ Northwest ☐ Southwest _____ Estimated travel time from home _____ Estimated expense of trip to school and back	Issues to consider: ■ Climate. If you're a warm-blooded type, you'll want to think twice before applying to a college in Alaska. ■ Proximity to home. Depending on your financial situation and your closeness to your family, a school that's far from home may be appealing or undesirable. Also, you may want to consider the ease with which you can reach you destination.	
School Charter (please ✓): ☐ State ☐ Private	State schools usually place more emphasis on your academic statistics (GPA, SAT scores, etc.) than on your personal qualities when making admissions decisions. In fact, some state schools do not require a personal essay. It is usually more difficult to get into a state school if you live out of state.	
Financial Considerations: _____ Annual tuition Scholarships available? ☐ Yes ☐ No	State schools are usually much less expensive than private schools, especially for in-state students, but do not always offer scholarships for any but the most needy students. If you can qualify for a scholarship at a private college, you may pay less than at a state school.	

School: _____

CHARACTERISTICS	COMMENTS	YOUR FEELINGS ABOUT EACH CHARACTERISTIC
Religious Orientation (please ✓): ☐ Nonsectarian ☐ Church affiliated Religious Affiliation: _____ _____	If you are applying to a nonsectarian school and your religious involvement is important to you, you may want to check into the kinds of religious organizations and activities that are available on campus or close by. If you are applying to a church-affiliated school, you may want to inquire whether religious courses or activities are compulsory.	
List your field(s) of interest: 1. _____ 2. _____ Number of courses offered: 1. _____ 2. _____ List special facilities, if applicable: _____ _____	Since going to college is primarily an academic experience, you will want to make sure you apply to schools that offer the courses and course-related facilities (e.g., laboratory, theater) you want. Colleges may also be curious about students who want to major in a field where the school's offerings are weak or nonexistent. You'll need to prepare an explanation.	
Academic Orientation: (please ✓): ☐ Liberal Arts ☐ Professional curriculum (e.g., engineering, accounting)	Some schools want to produce "generalists." Others are more interested in training students to be professionally skilled upon graduation. Your goals for your college education should match the orientation of the school.	

School: _____

CHARACTERISTICS	COMMENTS	YOUR FEELINGS ABOUT EACH CHARACTERISTIC
School Calendar (please ✓): ☐ Semester ☐ Trimester ☐ Quarter ☐ "Jan-Plan" or "interim term" ☐ Other	If you are interested in graduating early or taking more courses than usual, you'll want to go to a school where year-round study is possible. If you need to earn money to help pay for college, you'll want a school with substantial vacations between terms.	
Grading System (please ✓): ☐ Grades (A-F) ☐ Pass/fail ☐ Other	Consider whether you need the structure of grades or the freedom of pass/fail to perform well academically.	
Who teaches undergraduate courses (please ✓): ☐ Professors ☐ Instructors ☐ Graduate students ☐ Visiting faculty members ☐ Other	Although famous professors may give a school or department a good reputation, these professors may not be the ones who actually teach the undergraduate courses. Rather, lower-level faculty members may do the teaching, allowing the big names the opportunity to pursue their research. In general, at a large university, you are less likely to be taught by tenured professors, especially in the first two years. A smaller college may have fewer big names, but the tenured faculty members are often experienced and committed teachers who enjoy working with undergraduates.	

School: _____

CHARACTERISTICS	COMMENTS	YOUR FEELINGS ABOUT EACH CHARACTERISTIC
Extracurricular activities and facilities: In the left-hand column, please check the activities you hope to pursue in college. In the right-hand column, check those that are offered by the school: **Activities you want:** (please ✓): School offers: ☐ Athletics (please list) ☐ _____ _____ ☐ Artistic: music, art, theater, dance, etc. ☐ ☐ Organizational: student government, politics ☐ ☐ Social service ☐ ☐ College yearbook/ newspaper ☐ ☐ Other ☐	If you want to pursue an extra-curricular activity, be sure: ▪ it is offered. Don't write an essay about how much you enjoy drama if the school does not provide this activity. If you do, the school has cause to wonder whether you really know anything about its programs. ▪ the activity is open to students at a variety of skill levels. If, for example, you want to play football but you don't qualify for a high-pressure varsity team, check to see if there is an intramural sports program available.	
Cultural activities offered (please ✓): ☐ On campus ☐ In town ☐ Nearby (one-hour commute) ☐ Must travel more than one hour	If cultural programs such as professional theater, art shows, and lecture series are important to you, check out how frequently they are offered and the degree of accessibility.	

School: _____

CHARACTERISTICS	COMMENTS	YOUR FEELINGS ABOUT EACH CHARACTERISTIC
Social Orientation (please ✓): ☐ Fraternity/sorority ☐ Social clubs ☐ Special interest clubs (e.g., women's center, intercultural center) ☐ Dormitory-centered social life	Since college is a social experience, you'll want to choose schools that provide opportunities for socializing in an atmosphere that feels comfortable to you. If you don't know whether you want to join a fraternity or sorority, consider a school that provides some options.	
Student Image (please ✓): ☐ Preppy ☐ Counterculture ☐ Jock ☐ Intellectual ☐ Combination ☐ Other	Look for a school where you can fit in socially. This does not mean, of course, that the student body should conform solely to your type. Instead, look for a school that offers the right mix of students for you. You may also want to check out ■ the amount of alcohol and drug usage on campus. ■ the amount of social pressure to drink or take drugs. ■ the amount of sexual activity among students. ■ the amount of tolerance for people's differences. If possible, it's a good idea to visit the campus or talk to students or recent graduates of the college to get an idea of what the social life is like. Comparative guides to the colleges may also be helpful in this regard.	

School: _____

CHARACTERISTICS	COMMENTS	YOUR FEELINGS ABOUT EACH CHARACTERISTIC
Living Arrangements: _____% of students living on campus Dorms: ☐ single-sex ☐ coed _____% of students living off campus ☐ Apartments ☐ Fraternity/sorority ☐ Living at home and commuting	Students are often so intent on getting into a particular school that they give little thought to where they will live. ■ Be sure to check out the type and amount of dormitory space. You may cherish your privacy and hate being in a suite or coed dorm. ■ If your school is in the inner city, be sure there are enough dorm rooms or university-monitored apartments for those who want them. ■ Some schools empty out on weekends because students commute home or visit other campuses. It can be depressing to live on campus at a commuter school, and if weekend road trips are the norm, think about whether you'll enjoy them—or enjoy staying behind by yourself.	

Overall Reaction: (NOTE: In this section, you should summarize your feelings about the school.)

Decision: (please ✓)   ☐ Apply   ☐ Don't apply

With this exercise under your belt, you probably have a better idea of what each college can offer you, and you may have even crossed off a few colleges from your list. Combined with what you learned in the first exercise, the information gleaned from this analysis can help you adjust what you want to say so that your reader will be more receptive to it.

Now it's time to move away from the theoretical and begin, in Chapter 6, to apply what you've learned directly to your application.

Chapter 6

Crystalizing Your Ideas for Your Long and Short Essay Questions

Now that you've analyzed yourself and your reader, and you've developed some strategies for projecting your best self on paper, you're ready to connect your ideas to produce imaginative and cohesive essays. In the first part of this chapter, you'll focus on how you can make meaningful connections between your experiences and personal qualities explored in previous chapters. You'll grapple with such issues as: "How can I prove I'm a certain type of person?"; "What does this particular experience say about the kind of person I am?"; and "How have I developed over the years into this kind of person?" In the second part of this chapter, you'll develop a system for distilling the conclusions you have reached about yourself in a central idea statement with supporting ideas for each of your essays.

MAKING CONNECTIONS BETWEEN YOUR EXPERIENCES AND PERSONAL QUALITIES

In the following pages, you'll be asked to participate in a series of written exercises which will probably seem unrelated to each other. Do them anyway! By the end of the chapter you'll see how these exercises come together to help you clarify what you want to say in your essays.

You're ready now to examine your experiences, abilities, and preferences in an effort to find cohesive patterns for presenting your ideas in your essays. The following exercises will work best if you give your mind a chance to make some creative connections between ideas.

THE PERSONAL QUALITIES COLLEGES LOOK FOR IN APPLICANTS

STEP 1

Directions: Begin by reading through the list of personal qualities colleges find desirable in the chart on pages 60–62 and place a check in the box next to each quality you believe describes you.

☐ Seriousness of Purpose (to pursue a college education):

_____

_____

☐ Intellectual Ability (to handle college level work):

_____

_____

☐ Intellectual Curiosity (about ideas, academic subjects, people, trends, etc.):

_____

_____

☐ Creativity (as reflected: (1) in the way your mind works to solve problems and/or (2) a talent in the arts such as theatre, music, writing, painting, dancing, etc.):

_____

_____

☐ Open-mindedness (to ideas, people, and circumstances different from your own):

_____

_____

☐ Maturity (as demonstrated by being responsible and trustworthy):

_____

_____

☐ Concern for Others (either by devoting time to social service activities such as tutoring or by being considerate and empathic to others' feelings):

_____

_____

☐ Initiative (as in the ability to start a project or take on a responsibility on your own):

_____

_____

☐ Enthusiasm (as demonstrated by your eagerness to engage in activities):

_____

_____

☐ Confidence (in your ability to handle difficult situations):

_____

_____

☐ Being Organized (as in the ability to stay on top of multiple tasks):

_____

_____

☐ Sense of Humor (as in your ability to either find humor in difficult situations or make others laugh):

_____

_____

☐ Diligence/Persistence (as demonstrated by your ability to stay with a task until you complete it):

_____

_____

☐ Leadership (as shown in your ability to inspire others to work together to reach a mutual goal):

_____

_____

☐ Risk Taking (as shown in your ability to deal with uncertainty in order to reach your goal):

_____

_____

☐ Insight (as reflected in your ability to use introspection to understand aspects of yourself, such as your preferences and your motivations):

_____

_____

☐ Optimism (as reflected in your ability to find positive aspects in seemingly negative situations):

_____

_____

☐ Compromise (as in your ability to be flexible in negotiating with others):

_____

_____

☐ Overcoming Adversity (as demonstrated by your resourcefulness in dealing with serious problems such as divorce, death, illness, etc.):

_____

_____

☐ Other:

_____

_____

That was easy, wasn't it?

STEP 2

Next, in the space provided below each box you checked, write down two or more experiences that prove you possess that particular quality. This step is not so easy, but with a little thought, and especially a review of your Personal Inventory in Chapter 4, you can do it.

So, if you checked off "creativity," for example, you might jot down on your chart:

1. I designed a new logo for the masthead of the school newspaper and

2. I figured out a new and more equitable way to give out assignments to reporters on the school newspaper.

In the first example, you show your artistic creativity; in the second, you show your ability to creatively solve a problem.

You may find that you can't think of any examples for some of the qualities you checked. When that happens, simply cross off those qualities and concentrate on the others. Sometimes it helps to think of yourself as a character in a book, such as Huckleberry Finn, and approach the analysis of character in much the same way you do in English class. In this case, instead of thinking about three experiences from the book that prove that Huck is a certain kind of character, try to identify two or three experiences from your own life to prove you are a certain kind of person.

TOPICS AND PERSONAL QUALITIES

STEP 3

Turn back to page 41 and write down the three topics you listed at the end of the Personal Inventory and write them in the left-hand column of the Topics and Personal Qualities chart below.

STEP 4

Then, in the right-hand column next to each topic, write down the qualities from the list on pages 60–62 that these topics demonstrate you possess. Let's say, for example, you listed the following three topics: "designing the new logo for the school newspaper," "achieving a black belt in Karate," and "being the oldest of five children in my family." Then, based on the list of qualities colleges are looking for, you might write down that: designing the logo showed "creativity," earning a black belt showed "perseverance," and being the oldest of five children showed "responsibility."

TOPIC

1. _____

_____

PERSONAL QUALITIES

■ _____

■ _____

■ _____

■ _____

■ _____

2. _____

_____

■ _____

■ _____

■ _____

■ _____

■ _____

3. _____

_____

■ _____

■ _____

■ _____

■ _____

■ _____

TOPIC   PERSONAL QUALITIES

4. _____   ■ _____

  _____   ■ _____

                                          ■ _____

                                          ■ _____

                                          ■ _____

You may have noticed that the two exercises are inverted on pages 60–62 and 63–64. In the first exercise, you studied your personal qualities to generate a list of experiences, and in the second exercise, you studied your experiences to generate a list of personal qualities. This process of working back and forth between your experiences and personal qualities can help you discover patterns for presenting your ideas in your essays.

SHOWING GROWTH OVER TIME

Since colleges are particularly interested in students who can demonstrate how they have grown, the next step will help you to examine your experiences and personal qualities for signs of how you have developed over time.

You'll notice that each arrow in the following chart is really a time-line, which enables you to plot your growth chronologically, from Time 1 through Time 3.

- You can begin your time-line in your childhood, work your way through your junior high years, and end in the present as a high school senior.

- You could focus exclusively on your high school years, with Time 1 in 9th grade, Time 2 in 10th and 11th grades, and Time 3 in 12th grade.

- Or, you could even project your time-line into the future, hypothesizing what you will be like when you are in college or even after you have graduated. The combinations of time-frames are limitless. Just be sure that you stick with three chronological points along the time-line.

■ Here is an example to give you a better idea of how to pull your ideas together on the time-line. Suppose you would like to show how you have become more confident over a period of time. You might start out telling how, in 8th grade, you rarely raised your hand in class or participated in school activities because you weren't sure of yourself. You could then move on in time to the 9th through 11th grades when you decided to overcome your problem. At this point you would put down examples of how you began slowly to assert yourself. Finally, as a senior, you could discuss how you feel so much more comfortable in groups and how proud you are to have been elected a student government representative.

Personal Quality: ___confidence___

Time 1	Time 2	Time 3
8th Grade	9th–11th Grades	12th Grade
I rarely raised my hand in class	I worked on overcoming this problem by ■ speaking with teachers about my problem ■ I forced myself to speak in one class each day	The problem is now behind me, and I enjoy being in groups now. ■ elected student government representative

Notice how this example does not end with you becoming president of the student government. Admissions committees are not looking for students who can produce "Hollywood" endings. Instead, they are looking for students who can show that they have succeeded in terms of the realistic goals they have set for themselves.

With all this information in mind, you are ready to fill in the time charts. To do this,

■ select two experiences and two personal qualities from the charts in this chapter and write them down on the appropriate lines above each arrow.

■ Then, for each experience or quality write down examples that show your growth in that area.

SHOWING GROWTH OVER TIME

(pick personal qualities from pages 60–62)

Personal Quality: _____

Time 1	Time 2	Time 3

Personal Quality: _____

Time 1	Time 2	Time 3

(pick personal qualities from pages 60–62)

Experience: _____

| Time 1 | Time 2 | Time 3 |

Experience: _____

| Time 1 | Time 2 | Time 3 |

By now, you're probably beginning to believe that you really do have something to say in an essay and that there is some logic inherent in your ideas. In fact, this exercise has probably helped you to produce units of ideas, such as—"two examples that prove I am creative"—that you can expand upon or even connect with other units to form the basis for your essay answer.

A BASIC APPROACH TO ANSWERING ESSAY QUESTIONS

Now that you know how to look for the connections between your ideas, you're ready to establish a basic approach to answering the essay questions posed by the schools to which you are actually applying. Since the techniques in this part of the chapter are so crucial to a well-thought-out essay, you'll want to repeat these steps for each of your long and short essay questions.

STEP 1

To begin, select an essay question from one of your applications and write the name of the school and the question on the next page. Please be sure to copy the question word for word so that you don't inadvertently change the meaning.

SCHOOL: _____

QUESTION:

_____

_____

_____

_____

_____

_____

_____

_____

_____

_____

_____

_____

STEP 2

Now imagine that you and an admissions officer from the college are standing at a street corner waiting for the light to change. When it does, you'll walk in different directions. But while you're waiting, the admissions officer asks you the question you wrote on page 68. Since the light will change in thirty seconds, you must get your point across concisely.

This question may have taken you by surprise—but don't worry. You really are prepared!

- Thanks to your "Personal Inventory," you have a variety of subjects to talk about.

- You've analyzed the school and yourself, so you know what you want, what the school wants, what you have to offer, and what the school has to offer.

- You've examined your experiences and personal qualities and discovered cohesive patterns for presenting your ideas.

- All this information has helped you select a topic and shape it so you can make a favorable impression on the admissions committee.

- So, with confidence, here's how to respond:

_____

_____

_____

_____

_____

_____

_____

Good going! Believe it or not, you've just written the central idea of your essay!

That was hard work, but before you relax and give yourself the afternoon off, you need to take another look at what you've written. Since admissions officers respond more favorably to real, live people than to categories or statistics, you'll want to make sure your essay reflects your personal qualities, especially the ones colleges admire.

STEP 3

To do this, go back to the list of personal qualities colleges look for in applicants on pages 60–62. In the space below, write down the qualities you checked on this list that are demonstrated in the statement you just wrote. Please remember that this list covers many but not all personal qualities colleges admire. Feel free to add others, if appropriate.

PERSONAL QUALITIES REFLECTED IN THE STATEMENT ABOVE

1. _____

_____

2. _____

_____

3. _____

_____

NOTE: If you've found that your statement does not suggest any of the personal qualities you checked on the list, STOP and REGROUP! Most likely, you will need to change your topic, your approach, or both.

STEP 4

While going through this exercise, you've had some time to reflect on your response to the admissions officer. Chances are, you'll want to make some changes. In the space below, please rework your statement, making sure it really says what you want.

Your revised response: _____

_____

_____

_____

_____

_____

_____

_____

Now, let's suppose the admissions officer finds your thirty-second response so intriguing that he or she decides to walk with you for a few blocks when the light changes.

When he or she says, "Can you explain or prove what you've just said?" you'll need to respond with a few key sentences that can back up your central idea.

STEP 5

Think about how you will support this central idea, and then write the supporting statements on page 72, one to a box. Depending on the depth of the question, you may want to add or delete boxes.

In the space beneath each of these statements, fill in the reasons, examples, or illustrations that back up each of these supporting points.

Statement that supports main idea:

Details go here:

Statement that supports main idea:

Details go here:

Statement that supports main idea:

Details go here:

While you've been sweating away on these exercises, you'll be pleased to know you've been making great progress in writing your essay! Not only have you written a statement of your central idea, but you have developed the content of your essay as well.

Chapter 7

Structuring Your Essay for Busy Readers

If you're worried about getting started on your essays, relax—you've already begun. By working through chapters 4, 5, and 6, you've actually completed the most difficult step in the writing process: creating a preliminary plan. Since a plan can establish the logic of your paper and help you write in an orderly manner, you'll want to prepare one for each of your essays.

The next three chapters will bring you step by step from a rough plan to a refined one, so when you actually sit down to write, you'll know what to say.

This chapter will cover the first step: structuring your essay, using either a "tight" or "loose" format.

When you consider how important it is for you to make a good impression and how tiring it must be for the admissions committee to read through stacks of application forms, transcripts, recommendations, and essays, you can see why you need to get your points across quickly and easily.

When you structure your essay well, you guide your reader from point to point, making it easier for him or her to pay attention and understand your ideas. Without structure, your reader may become confused, lose interest, and stop reading altogether.

To show you how readers typically react to poorly structured essays, let's peek into the mind of an admissions officer as he reads the following essay:

ESSAY

"Pretty dull."

I have enjoyed these last years of high school. The courses I have taken have expanded my knowledge and have been fun. To many people, learning and fun are far from the same thing. However, I have found that learning can be made to be fun as well as hard work.

"So, this must be the thesis statement. It's not profound, but at least its here."

"Let's see. Biology must be the first example that shows how learning can be fun and hard work."

Biology has captivated me for as long as I can remember. Biology has always interested me because it is the ultimate feat of nature. Nature, meaning the universe, has reached a pinnacle of life, and that is what makes it so fascinating. The study of life is like a captivating and infinitely large puzzle.

"Hold it! What's this discussion of nature doing here?"

"Interesting image"

"In addition to what?"

In addition, in the past three years at high school, I have been taught philosophy in English and in history. In English we acquire the skill of finding the meaning of a book. Through this process, I have learned some philosophy as well as how to use language concisely and lucidly (I hope). In history, I have developed an interest in politics and world affairs.

"I'm lost. Where do philosophy, English, and history fit in?"

"Certainly not showing in this essay."

"So??? What's your point!"

"Good! We're back to the main point."

Being in class is not the only important aspect of my life nor do I want it to become the most important in college. Thus, I do not want to be in a school where there is so much competition between students that one student destroys another's work to get ahead. This is not my idea of healthy competition, and unfortunately, it seems to happen in a large number of colleges.

"Oh no. Not another unrelated idea."

"Now, what was this kid trying to say?"

Since this essay was so poorly constructed and lifeless, the reader became increasingly irritated with the amount of time and energy he put into deciphering it. As a result, the student not only lost a prime opportunity to sell himself to the admissions committee, but he may have also lost his reader's goodwill.

To make sure you don't suffer the same fate as this student, let's review the components of structure. First, we'll look at techniques and examples of "tightly" structured essays. Then we'll look at techniques and examples of "loosely" structured essays. Since both of these formats are equally effective and respected essay forms, feel free to choose whichever format best suits your material and your personal writing style.

THE TIGHTLY STRUCTURED ESSAY

A "tightly" structured essay should look very familiar to you. This is the format that your English teachers have been drumming into your head as early as fifth or sixth grade. All those "Five Paragraph Essays" you were forced to write included the basic components of this form:

- an introductory paragraph that leads you to your thesis statement

- three supporting paragraphs, each with a topic sentence and examples that develop the thesis statement, and

- a concluding paragraph that sums up the points in the essay and brings the essay to a satisfying close.

Let's take a look at the elements of a tightly structured essay.

The Thesis Statement

The thesis statement sets forth the central idea of your essay. Since the thesis holds the essay together, every point you make should support or develop it in some way. So, if your thesis states:

> I feel more confident in my ability to adjust to new situations as a result of having moved seven times in the last ten years.

then every idea in your essay should be directed toward establishing this point.

If you can't distill your thesis to a sentence or two, chances are your thoughts are still fuzzy. Rather than subject your reader to a blur of sentences, it's best to stop and think some more.

The Preview Statement

The preview statement immediately follows the thesis and shows the reader specifically how the thesis will be developed. In addition, it can help clarify and limit the thesis idea and tell the reader what to expect in the body of the essay as well. While a preview statement is not essential, it is particularly helpful when an essay develops more than one idea.

Here's a good example of a preview statement that could follow the above thesis:

> What has made each move easier is my awareness that schools are basically the same and that some kids are more receptive to new students than others.

This well-written preview statement alerts the reader to the two topics that will support the central idea: schools and students. It flows easily from the thesis without hitting the reader over the head with such juvenile phrasing as:

> I will develop three main points: first, . . . second, . . . and third. . . .

Topic Sentences

The topic sentence sets forth the main idea for each paragraph. A good one tells more than just what the topic will be. So, instead of merely saying,

> "Each school I attended was so different,"

a more telling topic sentence would state,

> "At first I was frightened of moving because each new school seemed like a foreign country."

In this case, the topic sentence actually says something about the topic. While the topic sentence usually occurs at the beginning of the paragraph, it can also be found in the middle or at the end.

Transitions

Transition statements form a bridge from one idea to another and help the reader follow your thought processes. A typical transition looks both backward and forward. First it refers to what has just been said and then it introduces the next idea. For example, your transition may say:

> Not only have I learned how to adjust to a new school, I have also learned how to make friends more easily.

In this case, the writer picks up the thread from the previous paragraph on adjusting to a new school and ties it in with the new paragraph on making friends.

The Concluding Statement

The concluding statement occurs in the last paragraph and alludes back to your main point. Without repeating your thesis word for word, the concluding statement ties your essay together and gives your reader a sense of completion. We will discuss concluding statements, as well as introductions, in depth, in chapter 8.

With the components of structure fresh in your mind, you're ready to examine an essay to see how it's put together. As you read the following essay, you'll notice that the thesis idea is applied to a single example.

Later, in another version of the same essay, you'll see how the writer expands the essay's focus by applying the thesis to more than one activity.

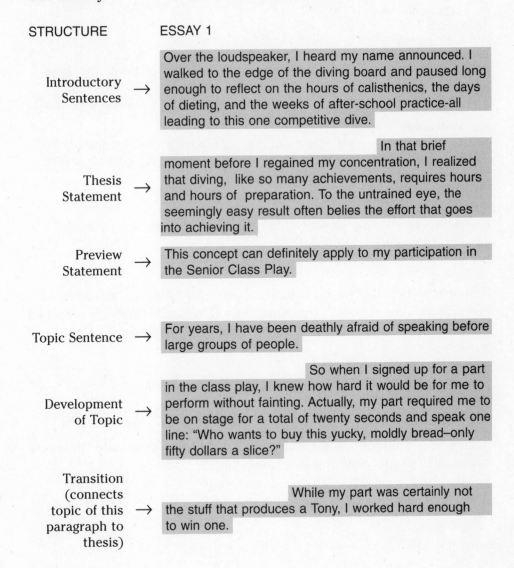

STRUCTURE

ESSAY 1

Introductory Sentences →

Over the loudspeaker, I heard my name announced. I walked to the edge of the diving board and paused long enough to reflect on the hours of calisthenics, the days of dieting, and the weeks of after-school practice-all leading to this one competitive dive.

Thesis Statement →

In that brief moment before I regained my concentration, I realized that diving, like so many achievements, requires hours and hours of preparation. To the untrained eye, the seemingly easy result often belies the effort that goes into achieving it.

Preview Statement →

This concept can definitely apply to my participation in the Senior Class Play.

Topic Sentence →

For years, I have been deathly afraid of speaking before large groups of people.

Development of Topic →

So when I signed up for a part in the class play, I knew how hard it would be for me to perform without fainting. Actually, my part required me to be on stage for a total of twenty seconds and speak one line: "Who wants to buy this yucky, moldly bread–only fifty dollars a slice?"

Transition (connects topic of this paragraph to thesis) →

While my part was certainly not the stuff that produces a Tony, I worked hard enough to win one.

STRUCTURE	ESSAY 1
Topic Sentence →	It seemed as if I practiced my one line forever.
Development of topic →	First, I recited it over and over again in the privacy of my room. Then, when I felt I had it under control, I invited my parents in for a preview. With their positive reinforcement and my increasing confidence, I took the bold step of asking some friends to watch "Sarah Heartburn" in the making. At school I practiced on stage before class during rehearsal, and sometimes even after the cast went home.
Transition (connects preceeding paragraph with text to come) →	Collectively, all this practice helped me on opening night.
Development of topic →	Of course, a part of me wanted to lie down and never get up, but I pulled myself together instead. In fact, I said my line so well that the audience actually laughed.
Concluding Statement (ties in with Thesis Statement) →	Although I was on stage for only a few seconds, I can honestly say that I worked toward this goal for several months.

For students wanting to write about a single experience or issue, this essay provides a good model.

The schematic diagram on the next page may help you visualize how the components of "tight" structure work to organize an essay with two or more topics. If you decide to write about multiple topics, you'll need to:

- list each topic in your preview statement, and
- make sure your thesis provides a logical link between topics.

Notice how the thesis and conclusion in the next essay hold the essay together the way bread holds a sandwich.

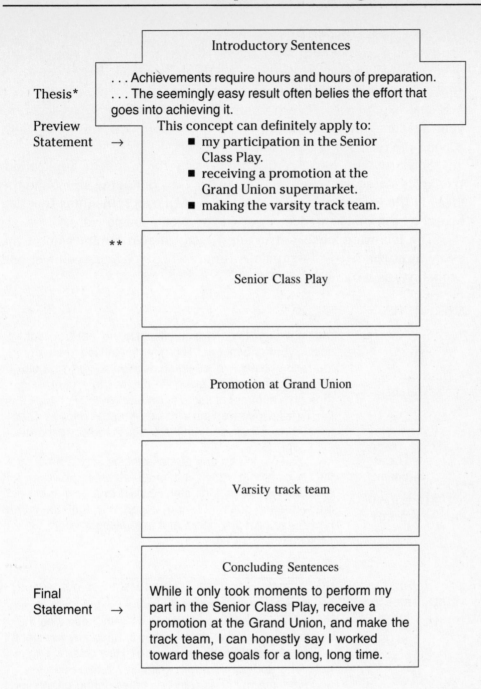

Introductory Sentences

Thesis*

. . . Achievements require hours and hours of preparation.
. . . The seemingly easy result often belies the effort that goes into achieving it.

Preview
Statement   →

This concept can definitely apply to:
- my participation in the Senior Class Play.
- receiving a promotion at the Grand Union supermarket.
- making the varsity track team.

**

Senior Class Play

Promotion at Grand Union

Varsity track team

Concluding Sentences

Final
Statement   →

While it only took moments to perform my part in the Senior Class Play, receive a promotion at the Grand Union, and make the track team, I can honestly say I worked toward these goals for a long, long time.

---

* Notice how the box for the thesis statement extends beyond the other boxes. The diagram is designed in this way so the thesis provides a visual umbrella for all the supporting ideas.

** Depending on the complexity of your essay, you may wish to provide one or more boxes for each of the main points you will be discussing.

THE "LOOSELY" STRUCTURED ESSAY

Reading an example of a "loosely" structured essay should bring back memories of stories you wrote in elementary school when you were encouraged to be creative and to write in the first person about your personal experiences. These essays frequently told a story and held your readers' attention because the story unfolded chronologically, leaving the reader in suspense until the end.

Similarly, in a loosely structured essay for a college application, the thesis statement seems to organically grow out of the story, and the ideas in the essay are moved along by well-placed transitions that can take the form of a sentence, a phrase, or even a single word.

The following loosely structured essay should remind you of the essay form you used to write so naturally when you were younger and probably less inhibited.

STRUCTURE	ESSAY 2
	"All right guys, underwear on first. No, no, no! Not your socks, your underwear." The guys I'm talking to are my fourteen hyperactive, attention deficient seven-year old boys who I have been given the dubious task of guiding through a summer of camp activities. When I first took this job, I envisioned working with kids who could follow directions, throw a ball, and run the bases in the correct order.
Introductory Sentences →	
Thesis Statement →	My kids couldn't do any of these things, at least not in the (beginning.) By the (end) of the summer, however, not only did I teach my kids athletic skills and how to cooperate with each other, but more importantly, they taught me how to connect with them and take pleasure from their achievements and growth.
◯ Transition Words	
Time 1; Topic Sentence →	As camp got under way, I found that I was not a good counselor. I was unhappy because I didn't have an athletic group. What was I going to do with these kids if they couldn't play sports? Was I going to have any fun since I couldn't let my athletic skills loose? How was I going to get along and connect with each kid? It had been pounded into my head a million times during orientation that counselors should find ways to create special bonds with each camper. I struggled with these questions and my attitude, which unfortunately focused on (my campers' shortcomings.)
◯ Transition Words	

STRUCTURE

ESSAY 2

Time 1 continued;

○ Transition Ideas

⟶ (Simultaneously) in another part of camp, Jim Robertson, the camp owner and director, was (concerned with my) (performance.) Jim runs his camp as if it were his own family. He wants both campers and staff to become the best people they can possibly be. Just as he encourages his counselors to support the campers, he and the other supervisors are committed to helping the staff grow. So, when Jim observed me, he saw me as a counselor struggling to reach my potential.

Time 2   ⟶   Two weeks into the summer, Jim pulled me aside to talk. I now consider that discussion to be the changing point of my summer. We discussed my concerns and expectations and what he was looking for in me as a counselor. Jim is a great motivator and gives good advice. He really got me thinking. Jim wanted me to succeed. If I succeeded then he succeeded. He not only told me to try to talk to my campers, but most importantly to listen to them so I could get to know what each of them is about. By plugging into their world, I found that I could actually be both seven and seventeen at the same time.

Time 2 continued;

○ Transition Word

⟶ I was (also) encouraged to learn from my co-counselor, Bill, who had six years of experience. From watching Bill and asking for his help, I learned a lot about the psychological aspects of the job. I soon realized that a tremendous amount of empathy is needed in order to be able to create an emotionally safe atmosphere for the kids. I particularly remember when Bill taught me this lesson. Our group was playing basketball and one of the boys blocked another camper's shot. I became openly excited about the great block the camper had just made. It was at that time that Brian came over to me. He asked me to consider how the kid whose shot had just been blocked might be confused if he saw his own counselor cheering. I quickly realized that the camper could be pondering if I thought he was a bad athlete or if I liked the other child better. By the end of the summer, I had learned to think ahead and to see the big picture so that I didn't create situations where a child might feel hurt.

Time 3   ⟶   As the summer came to an end, I had become a happy and involved counselor. I was successful at making personal connections with each child in my group. I had learned to like and respect them as individuals. As I became more engaged with my campers, they became more attached to me. Campers from other groups, not just mine, would look forward to seeing me and would (run to greet me in the morning.)

A Word About Length

*I*n addition to structuring your essay, it's important to consider your essay's length. The general rule is to keep your answer within the space allotted on the application, no matter how small that space might be. One reason for this restriction is that admissions people want to keep a lid on the number of words they must read. In addition, they're interested in seeing how concisely you can express complex ideas.

Sometimes an application will allow you to continue your essay on additional pages. If this is the case, limit your answer to one or two extra pages at the most. While your readers want to know something about you, they're certainly not interested in reading your full-length autobiography!

STRUCTURE   ESSAY 2

Time 3 →   I had a positive impact on most of my campers. Par-
continued;   ents saw changes in their children's athletic skills and
                    attitudes toward sports. I had learned to be patient so
◯ Transition   that I could help to develop their skills. I am particularly
Ideas   proud of my work with Mike, who at the beginning of the
                    summer was afraid to put his face in the water. When the
                    summer had ended, Mike had earned five swimming
                    badges under my care. Two sets of parents were so
                    pleased with their child's progress that they asked me if I
                    would work with their children during the school year. I
                    am currently working with their children, helping to de-
                    velop their athletic skills, which I hope will also lead to
                    their increased self-esteem.

                    My summer at Camp Redwood has opened up a whole
                    realm of possibilities for me. Through my kids, I have
◯ Transition   discovered that I really like children, I really like teaching
Ideas   children, and I enjoy being good at what I like.

As seen in this example, the "loosely" structured essay follows the rules of basic structure. However, it relies strongly on two techniques for its effectiveness:

- the chronological order of ideas and events and

- emphasis on transitional sentences, phrases, and words to connect ideas.

You'll notice that this essay does not need a preview statement to be coherent.

NOW IT'S YOUR TURN

In chapter 6, you wrote a response to a question posed by an admissions officer. In that answer, you clarified the central idea of your essay. Now you're ready to rework your answer, focusing your attention on structure.

In the space below, copy your revised response from page 71.

_____

_____

_____

_____

_____

_____

Now, in this space, rework your response so it includes a thesis that sets forth the central idea (and a preview statement that prepares the reader for what is to come in the rest of the essay, if you're writing a "tightly" structured essay).

_____

_____

_____

_____

_____

The following diagram is designed to accommodate your ideas whether you choose to use a "tight" or "loose" format.

- To begin, refer to the completed diagrams on page 77 for examples.

- Next, fill in your central idea or thesis statement, followed by your preview if you're using a "tight" structure.

- The middle boxes can be filled out chronologically or topically, depending on your type of structure.

- Then, insert your supporting points, referring back to your ideas in Chapter 6, page 72.

- Finally, write a concluding sentence or phrase that ties your ideas together.

Write your
introductory
sentences here.   →

Write your
thesis   →
statement
here.

Write your preview
statement here.   →

Write your first
main point here.   →

Write your second
main point here.   →

Write your third
main point here.   →

Write a concluding
statement here.   →

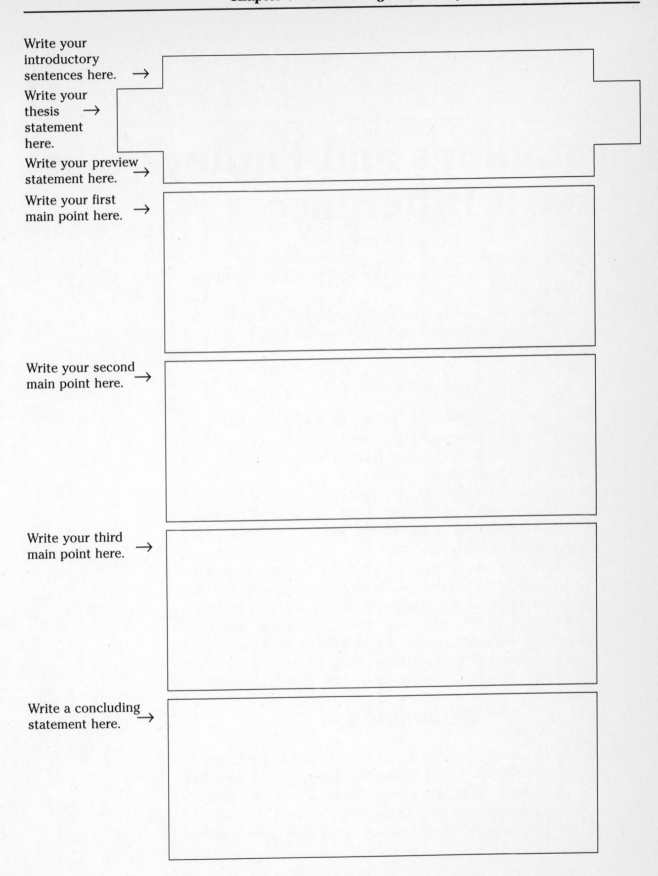

Chapter 8

Beginnings and Endings Can Make a Difference

Question: When is a beginning an ending?
 Answer: When an admissions officer can't get beyond the first few sentences of your essay.

Question: When does the conclusion mean "you're finished"?
 Answer: When the admissions committee can't remember you or what you wrote.

First words are often the last. If they're boring, confusing, or irrelevant, readers are quick to put them down. If your conclusion drifts off into space or ends abruptly, your readers may stop reading just when you hope to convince them to admit you.

To avoid losing your readers at either end, your first sentences should grab their attention and lead them into the heart of the essay. Your conclusion should refocus the readers' attention on the essential ideas and provide a feeling of closure.

On the following pages, you'll be introduced to some techniques that can get you off to a good start and bring you to a successful close. As you study the examples, you'll probably find at least one beginning and ending that works well with your material and that you'll feel comfortable using. But keep in mind that this list is not exhaustive. If your material suggests an idea not listed here, feel free to try it out. These techniques may inspire you to experiment on your own.

BEGINNINGS

With a good beginning, you can wake up your readers and get them to focus on you in a positive way. To achieve this result, your beginning must grab your readers' attention first and then lead your readers directly to the main point of your essay. While each of the following examples differs in approach, each one is successful because it follows this prescription.

1. MAKING A REFERENCE TO A FAMILIAR OCCASION

Your readers are likely to perk up when you mention an occasion or incident they recognize.

STRUCTURE	EXAMPLE	COMMENTS
Attention Device	For most of my life, Veterans' Day has meant little more than parades, flags, and a day off from school. This year, however, my attitude has taken a more serious tone as a result of a course I took on modern warfare.	Veteran's Day has a high recognition quotient because: 1. it is a national holiday, and 2. it occurs in the fall when admissions officers begin to read applications. This introduction is effective because: 1. it gains attention, and 2. shows off two personal traits admissions people seek in applicants: ■ growth ■ sensitivity
Main Point of Essay		

2. ASKING QUESTIONS

The use of questions in an introduction can be effective because it rouses the reader's curiosity. To use this technique effectively, be sure to (1) provide answers in the body of your essay for any questions you pose and (2) limit the number of questions to two or three. If you ask more, you run the risk of becoming repetitive and boring.

STRUCTURE	EXAMPLE	COMMENTS
Attention Device	Imagine you're an editor for the high school yearbook and you discover after doing some opinion research that sales are down and student apathy is up. What would you do to increase sales? Would you revamp the format or stick to the traditional approach? How would you get the support of the faculty and administration on any changes you might suggest? These are three questions I had to answer as I worked on the yearbook this fall.	This introduction immediately gets the readers' attention because it involves him or her in the writer's situation. The three questions further involve the reader.
Main Point: The three questions constitute the main point and give structure to the essay. The writer will devote a separate section to answering each question in the body of the essay.		

3. TELLING A NARRATIVE

Since everyone enjoys a story, a narrative is a good way to begin your essay. For this approach to work, however, the narrative should be specific and easy to follow, create suspense, and lead the reader directly into the heart of the subject.

STRUCTURE	EXAMPLE	COMMENTS
Attention Device	I remember the first time I tried a scientific experiment. The kid next door had one of those do-it-yourself kits. No one was home, and we set up shop. We were too sophisticated to read the manual, so we made our own concoctions using a little of this and a little of that. We held our secret formula over a flame, bringing it to a boil, and waited, and waited—and waited.	The storylike quality of this beginning grabs the reader's attention. The suspense maintains the attention. The ending of the narrative gives the reader a pleasant surprise and primes the reader for the main point. The main point suggests the student is goal-oriented and disciplined.
Main Point of Essay	Since then I have learned that if I really want something to happen, I have to plan and work for it. As a result of this lesson, I have planned and worked to become a counselor in the county's peer counseling program.	
The Preview Statement shows the reader how the student specifically will develop his thesis.		

4. GIVING FACTS OR DETAILS

When details or facts are interesting, they can do a good job of grabbing your readers' attention. Keep in mind, however, that too many facts or details can bore your readers or make them grow impatient as they wait for you to show how the facts relate to the main point of your essay.

STRUCTURE	EXAMPLE	COMMENTS
Attention Device	I've always been impressed by people who have made great achievements at an early age: Alexander Hamilton was Lieutenant Colonel at twenty, a framer of the U.S. Constitution at thirty, and Secretary of the Treasury at thirty-two. Alexander Graham Bell invented the telephone at twenty-eight, and George Eastman produced dry plates for photography at twenty- six. Although my parents and teachers coax me to slow down. I'm eager to make my mark as soon as possible.	This statement sets the stage for the facts that follow. These statements are interesting because they present little-known facts about well-known people. In this statement, the student implies his enthusiastic outlook and his desire to achieve.
Main Point of Essay		

5. QUOTATIONS

If you can find an appropriate quotation to illustrate or lead into the main point of your essay, a quotation can be an effective opening. Unfortunately, students are often indiscriminate in their selection, picking quotes that are either unrelated to their topic or just plain trite. If you decide to use this approach, be sure to select a quotation that is pertinent to your subject and enables you to move gracefully into your introduction.

STRUCTURE	EXAMPLE	COMMENTS
Attention Device	"I wish you wouldn't squeeze so," said the Dormouse, who was sitting next to her. "I can hardly breathe." "I can't help it," said Alice very meekly: "I'm growing." —Lewis Carroll, *Alice in Wonderland*	This is an appealing quotation because it deals with the subject of personal growth in a whimsical way.
Transition: to make the transition, the student echoes the words "I'm growing" from the quotation with the phrase "while we all grow" in her essay. *Main Point of Essay*	While we all grow at different rates, I feel a special affinity for Alice, who grew at an astonishing rate all of a sudden. In the first few months of my senior year, I feel I have changed and accomplished more than I have in my freshman, sophomore, and junior years put together.	The student connects the quotation to her essay by following up on the theme of growth.
Preview Statement: this sentence specifically shows the reader how the student will develop her thesis.	In this short time I feel I have become a better student, a better athlete, and a happier person.	

ENDINGS

Since the essay is one of the few opportunities you'll have to distinguish yourself from the pool of applicants, you'll want to be sure your conclusion makes a coherent and positive impression. With a good ending, you can round out your essay, tie in new ideas, and provide a lasting impact so the admissions committee won't forget your points or you.

Three of the most effective ways to consolidate your ideas and provide a note of finality are:

- a summary,

- a summary plus a look into the future, and

- a further implication of the essay idea.

These three approaches are particularly well suited to essays for college applications because they focus your reader on your thoughts rather than on stylistic gimmicks.

On the following pages, you can get an idea of how these conclusions work.

SAMPLE INTRODUCTION

Below is a sample introduction. On the following pages, you'll find three possible conclusions to go with this introduction—one for each of the three types of conclusions mentioned above.

In 2000, Ralph Nader took a great political and personal risk by deciding to run for President of the United States as a candidate on the Green Party ticket. Without the support of a major political party, however, Nader was destined to fail.

While high school politics may not compare in scope to national politics, I believe I faced an equally difficult situation when I ran for senior class President without the support of influential students. Although I lost the election, the satisfaction I received from standing by my convictions made the effort worthwhile.

CONCLUSION I: SUMMARY

A summary rephrases the main ideas of your essay to keep them fresh in your reader's mind.

STRUCTURE	EXAMPLE	COMMENTS
Transition	Although my campaign for class president was a lonely one, I believe the time and effort that went into that campaign helped me to grow. I have learned that I possess an inner strength that allows me to go on with my everyday life even while I'm facing anxiety and uncertainty. And perhaps more importantly, I have learned the value of standing by my convictions, even if it means going against the crowd.	This summary is effective because it draws together the main points without sounding like a laundry list or repeating word for word what was said in the introduction.
Main Ideas		

CONCLUSION II: SUMMARY AND PREDICTION

By adding a prediction to a summary, you move the essay idea into the future. This approach is especially effective for college applications because it can help your reader see how you might perform or contribute to life on campus in the next few years. If your prediction projects far enough into the future, it can give your readers a glimpse of what you might be like when you finish college.

STRUCTURE	EXAMPLE	COMMENTS
Summary	Although my campaign for class president was a lonely one. I believe the time and effort that went into that campaign helped me grow. I have learned I possess an inner strength that allows me to go on with my everyday life even while I'm facing anxiety and uncertainty. And perhaps more importantly, I have learned the value of standing by my convictions, even if it means going against the crowd.	
Prediction	As I grow older, I will have to take other stands that may be unpopular, but I am confident that I will become increasingly adept at handling peer pressure.	With this prediction, the student projects into the future, where she sees herself handling difficult interpersonal situations with increasing finesse. In most cases, the reader will be impressed with the student's ability to grow and her optimistic outlook.

CONCLUSION III: A FURTHER IMPLICATION OF THE ESSAY IDEA

This type of conclusion rounds out the essay by enlarging its scope. If you select this approach, make sure you don't introduce ideas that need to be developed in additional paragraphs.

STRUCTURE	EXAMPLE	COMMENTS
Transition	Making the decision to run for class president on an unpopular platform was difficult. Although I feel I did what was best for me, a part of me wonders what would have happened if I had not run. That is what makes decisions so difficult. You have to choose; you can't have it all.	This conclusion increases the scope of the essay by viewing the school election as just one of the many choices competing for the student's time and energy.
Further Implication of Essay Idea		The reader does not feel the need for further explanation of the enlarged essay idea because the last two sentences create a note of finality.

Now that you know what makes a beginning and ending striking and meaningful, you're ready to apply your knowledge to your own essays.

In the space below, rework the introductory paragraph you wrote on page 83 in Chapter 7. In this effort, you'll want to write an engaging introduction without sacrificing structure. As you write, remember to:

- grab your reader's attention,

- lead your reader to the main point of your essay, and

- write a preview statement that shows the reader more specifically how you'll develop your thesis.

Introduction:

_____

_____

_____

_____

_____

_____

_____

_____

_____

_____

Now, in this space write a draft of your conclusion, making sure it creates a positive impact and is consistent with the ideas established in the first paragraph. Be aware, however, that this conclusion may change when you write a draft of your entire essay. Until then, this version will help crystalize your ideas and give you an idea of how your essay will end.

Conclusion:

_____

_____

_____

_____

_____

_____

_____

_____

_____

_____

_____

_____

Some Endings to Avoid

*S*ince weak endings can dilute the impact of even the best essays, here are some tips on what to avoid:

■ *Rehashing Old Points*
   If you summarize ideas that are obvious or reargue points you've already established, you could be guilty of rewriting the body of your essay in your conclusion. In the case of essays for college admission, making your point once is usually enough.

■ *Going on to a New Point*
   A conclusion should draw together what you've already said. If a new idea relating to your central idea pops into your head as you write your conclusion, you'll need to decide if the point enhances what you've already written. If yes, work the idea into the body of your essay; if no, leave it out.

■ *Making False Conclusions*
   Readers, especially busy ones, look forward to conclusions. To tell them you're going to end and then keep going is like telling marathon runners they have crossed the finish line when in fact they have five more miles to go. Since most readers will react with frustration to a false ending, don't say you're going to stop unless you mean it.

■ *Obvious Endings*
   Try to avoid hitting your reader over the head with phrases such as "In conclusion," "To sum up," or "As you can see." These phrases are too heavy-handed; your readers should be able to tell that you are making your concluding remarks without being told. Since your essay is in part a sample of your writing ability, your reader will be looking for signs that you can write at a college level.

■ *Tacked-on Endings*
   Since good endings are so difficult to write, many people just tack on a couple of sentences to the last paragraph and hope they'll do. Unfortunately, these sentences usually have no relationship to the ideas that precede them, and they can have a jarring effect on the reader.
   The worst offender in this category goes something like this: "For all these reasons, I want to go to Cornell University"—or Penn State or Beloit College or whatever school the student is applying to at the time.
   Not only does this ending sound tacked on, it's tack-y! Any admissions officer will realize the student is simply filling in the blanks. While you may desperately want to go to a particular school, your reader may never get beyond the insincerity of your last sentence.

Chapter 9

How to Keep Your Reader Reading

QUESTION: What's wrong with this essay?

> For a seventeen-year-old person applying to college, the future appears to be bursting with numerous and diverse opportunities. I am excited about my future, for though I am certain I will do my utmost to create a successful and happy one, it is uncertain what it will be exactly. I am certain, however, that a strong liberal arts education will help to shape my future and stretch my mind and talents to hone my intellect and wit.

ANSWER: It's boring!

Actually, it's more than boring. In this single effort, the student manages to build a wall between himself and the reader. Although the student expresses confidence and enthusiasm about his future, he fails to articulate what his goals are, how he intends to achieve them, and how a liberal arts education will help. As a result, the reader gets no sense of what the student is like and what he hopes to accomplish in college. The vague, glib tone of this essay frustrates the reader's efforts to form a relationship with the student.

To keep your reader reading, here are some tips on how to make the tone and style right.

TONE

You wouldn't come right out and say to an admissions officer: "I'm terrific and you're stupid." or "I'm desperate, so please take me." Yet admissions officers frequently "hear" these messages in the tone of the essay.

Although students don't usually set out to make inappropriate statements, their word choice and phrasing often misrepresent the attitudes they hold toward themselves and their readers. As a result, it is entirely possible for a student to believe her essay exudes enthusiasm while the reader perceives the student to be pompous and pushy.

When readers "hear" an inappropriate, negative, or extreme tone, they frequently take revenge by tuning out or even lowering their opinion of the student.

Obviously, you won't want to face either of these consequences. So to make sure your tone is on target, take some time to study the following list of desirable and undesirable tones.

Tones to Strive for

- *Friendliness:* Admissions people respond favorably to warm, approachable applicants. To set this tone, you'll want to show a willingness to reveal something of yourself without unburdening your soul to the reader.

- *Confidence:* Since people gravitate to those who feel good about themselves, you'll want your reader to sense your confidence and personal satisfaction. However, don't overdo it.

- *Enthusiasm:* Enthusiasm is contagious. Your reader is likely to perk up if you can express your genuine excitement for your topic.

- *Respect for Authority:* Admissions people have a well-tuned ear for deference. Your words should let your reader know you're aware of his or her power to admit or reject you.

Tones to Avoid

- *Groveling:* It's one thing to show respect; it's another thing to grovel. If you don't think highly of yourself, your reader won't either. So avoid any pleading or self-deprecating words. After all, you're an applicant, not a supplicant.

- *Antagonism:* If you criticize or attack your reader, be prepared for trouble. No matter how brilliant your argument may be, your reader will miss its merits if he feels you're out to get him. Remember, you want to woo your reader, not inspire his wrath.

■ *Whining:* No one likes a whiner. If you whine or grumble on your application about your grades, your teachers, or why you're not number one in your class, your reader will assume you'll whine and grumble at college as well.

Humor: A Word of Caution

Many students believe they'll win their readers over if they keep the tone light and witty. To be sure, humor is a delightful way to engage your reader—but only if your writing is truly funny. Since you can't know for certain whether your reader shares your sense of humor, be aware that you take a risk if you try to be funny on your college application.

Making Sure Your Tone Is on Target

Knowing which tones to use and using them effectively are two different things. Here are some techniques to help you get the tone right:

■ Picture yourself talking to an admissions officer. If you were face-to-face, would you actually say what you've just written? When your spoken essay doesn't sound right to you, chances are the tone is off.

■ Now, imagine you are the admissions officer. You're looking for quality students, you're under pressure to find them, and you're probably tired from reading so many applications. You sit down to read your essay. How do you react?

■ As a final check, get an outside opinion. Try to find a reader who can be objective about you and what you've written. A teacher is usually a good candidate for this job. Ask your reader to look over your essay, keeping an ear tuned for tone. If he or she has any doubts or negative reactions, ask her to identify the source of the problems. Then it is up to you to correct them.

STYLE

Since your writing style, like your tone, can make a difference in how a reader feels about you, take the time now to review some principles of good writing.*

Use Vivid Descriptions

Your experiences will seem more lifelike to your reader if you describe the events vividly and concretely. In the following example, a student describes an important event in such a matter-of-fact way that the reader is tempted to shrug and say, "So what?"

---

*For an interesting and concise review of style, please see Strunk and White, *The Elements of Style* (New York: The Macmillan Co., 1979).

Whenever I make a commitment, I stand by it. Last year I had a major role in a school play, and although I had the flu, I went on with the show.

Now, let's take the same passage and pump some life into it:

Whenever I make a commitment, I stand by it. Last year I had a major role in a school play. Two nights before the opening, however, I came down with the flu. To be honest, I don't remember feeling so sick in all my life. My head ached, my bones creaked, and my eyes drooped. But I was determined to appear on stage, even if I was half-dead.

On opening night, I dragged myself out of bed, struggled into my costume, painted my face, and stepped out on stage. I knew my dramatic performance would not be as good as it could be, but I knew my personal performance deserved a Tony award.

In this version of the tale, the reader can share in the student's experiences. The reader sees the student's discomfort; she sees the student preparing to go on stage. The result is an involved reader who is more able to care about and remember the student. Be careful, however, not to go on and on. Too much description can be just as boring as too little description.

Use Exact Words

Exact words convey exact meanings, and it's your job to find the words that say precisely what you mean. Every time you put down a vague word or phrase, force yourself to be specific. Don't say, for example, "The trip was good" when you really mean "The trip was informative," or "I looked in the library for a book" when you can evoke a more precise picture with "I scoured the library for a book." Precise language can also help you cut down on excess verbiage. Frequently you can find one or two specific words that suffice for five vague ones.

Use Fresh and Forceful Language

When writers become lazy, they frequently allow their language to lapse into clichés. Some writers use clichés because they can't hear the difference between a hackneyed expression and a fresh and powerful one.

For example, the student who wrote the following passage sincerely believed that she was expressing her deepest thoughts in a profound and original way. Instead, she glides from one trite expression to the next (the clichés are underlined):

We have all grown closer together and share a very special relationship. We have learned to make every day count and not let any precious time slip away. We need to live and enjoy life now, while we still can.

To avoid the cliché trap, double-check your sentences for phrases that sound too slick or pat. Instead of being smooth and elegant, these passages just might be worn-out phrases your ear has become used to hearing.

Vary Sentence Type and Length

Readers crave variety. When they're confronted with a series of short, simple sentences or long, complicated ones, they usually react in the same way: they become frustrated and bored.

In the following example, the student writes six sentences, all simple and declarative. None contain more than eleven words nor less than seven:

> I am a member of the school band. I started to play trumpet in sixth grade. I played the trumpet in junior high school and high school. The band plays at all the varsity games. The band also plays at special city events. We play in the Memorial Day parade.

Not only is the sameness stifling, but the choppiness of the short sentences leaves the reader exhausted.

Now, let's go to the other extreme. Here the student transposes those six sentences into a long, complicated one:

> I started to play trumpet in the sixth grade and have continued playing in the junior and senior high school band, which plays at all high school games and city events such as the Memorial Day parade.

Since too much of one thing is too much, try to write paragraphs that include a mix of long and short, simple and complex sentences. In this way, you'll have a better chance of maintaining your reader's attention and interest.

Use the Active Voice

You've heard it all before: active sentences are vibrant and alive; passive sentences are dull and dead. Take a look, for example, at the following sentences:

> Baseball has always been a great love of mine. Whenever the plate is approached, the pitcher is stared in the eye, and the bat is furiously swung at the ball, this incredible feeling comes over me.

With a lifeless and awkward statement like this, the student may never get to first base. First of all, the reader is not certain who is doing the "approaching," "staring," or "swinging." Is it the student or some imaginary ball player?

Clarity aside, this sentence strikes out because the student fails to convey the excitement he or she feels for the sport. In fact, these sentences paint the picture of a player hanging around waiting for the action to happen to him.

When the student rewrites the sentences in the active voice, with the ball player actively engaged in making contact with the ball, the sentence comes to life and so does the reader:

> Boy, do I love baseball! I get a heady feeling whenever I approach the plate, stare the pitcher in the eye, and swing my bat with all my might.

Although active sentences are usually better than passive, students often gravitate to the passive voice because they believe it makes their writing sound more mature. In reality, the passive voice distances the reader from the writer and can even make the reader feel shut out. This is a reaction you'll obviously want to avoid. To help bring your reader in closer to you, to help him or her share your experiences, write in the active voice.

Use the Personal Voice

There are only so many themes in life, and admissions officers have read about them all. Students write about how they have changed, overcome, won, and learned. They tell about their summer trips, their work experiences, their most exciting, interesting, or challenging moments in life. If the answers are all the same, you may wonder why do you have to bother with the questions at all? Because you are not the same as any other candidate applying to college, and the admissions committee is hoping that you will write in a way—using a personal voice—that will make a universal story your own.

When you write in a personal voice, you are expressing your thoughts in your own words, in a way that only you can say them. In addition to finding the uniqueness about an incident, you are looking for the expression that comes from your heart as well as your head. If you tap into this reservoir of thought and feeling, you can be sure that no one else can possibly describe an experience in the same way as you.

Now that you've completed a detailed plan, with some attention to structure, beginnings, endings, tone, and style, you're ready to write a rough draft of your essay. In the next chapter, you'll get some pointers on how to relieve the stress that is often associated with writing.

Chapter 10

Overcoming Fear of the Blank Page

For most writers, nothing can bring on a case of self-doubt quite as quickly as a blank page. But since you've already worked out a detailed plan complete with introduction, development, and conclusion, you can confidently begin to write your rough draft. To help you concentrate, you'll want to limit any interruptions that could cause you to lose your train of thought.

If your home is filled with distractions such as younger siblings slamming doors or playing radios at ear-shattering levels, try to enlist your family's cooperation. If you can't change their habits, change yours by writing at odd hours when family members are out or asleep. And if all else fails, look for another place to work, such as a library.

Distractions, however, do not always come from the outside. Sometimes writers interrupt themselves, especially when they try to write a rough draft and polish it at the same time. Writing like this is analogous to driving with your feet on the gas and brake pedals simultaneously. As a writer or a driver, you won't get far!

So even if your sentences are ragged or your words imprecise, force yourself to continue down the page. Later, when all your ideas are on paper, you can go back to smooth out the sentences and find that perfect word.

When you finish your rough draft, you will probably feel both pleased and relieved. Your hard work deserves recognition, and you should give yourself a pat on the back and a rest.

Giving yourself a rest is particularly important. Not only does it allow you to unwind, but it gives you a chance to gain some objectivity about what you've just written. If you try to be critical too soon, you

Tips for Overcoming Writer's Block

*I*f *you have trouble getting started or if you get stuck along the way, here are some tips to help you get going:*

■ *START ANYWHERE*
There's no law that says you must write the introduction first, the middle part next, and the conclusion last. Instead, you can start with the part that's easiest for you. This could be a section that you know the most about or that particularly interests you. In most cases, the confidence you'll gain from completeing this section will give you the push you need to write the rest.

■ *CREATE A DEADLINE*
If you work well under pressure, you can pretend you must hand in to a teacher a section of your essay in thirty to forty minutes. Sometimes an artificial deadline such as this can create just enough urgency to snap your thoughts into place.

■ *TALK TO AN IMAGINARY LISTENER*
If your words won't flow because your thoughts are muddy, try explaining your ideas to an imaginary listener. This technique works best if you visualize a person sitting next to you and you say aloud: "What I'm really trying to say is . . ."

■ *FREE WRITE FOR TEN MINUTES*
Sometimes the sheer act of writing can help you clarify your ideas and formulate your words. For this exercise to work, you need to set aside ten minutes to do nothing but write. If you can, stay with your topic. But, if you can't, write about anything-even the weather. The important thing is to keep writing and avoid any interruptions that could hinder your flow of thought, such as criticizing what you've written or checking your watch.

may mistake what you think you said for what is really on paper. Since sentences that appeared crystal clear to you just after you wrote them will often seem confused and garbled later, it's a good idea to give yourself some time before you begin to revise.

The amount of time you need to become objective about your work depends largely upon the amount of time you have to meet deadlines. If your applications are not due for several weeks, you can afford to put your essay down for a few days while you begin work on another. But if you have a week or less, you might be able to devote only half a day or just a few hours to gain that much-needed objectivity.

Whatever your schedule, don't mistake this interlude as a license to procrastinate. If you put your essays down for too long, you may lose your momentum, making it harder for you to get started again.

Once you've gained your objectivity, you'll probably reread what you've written and exclaim: "I can't believe I wrote that!" or "I'm so glad I didn't send this out!" Even if you're pleased with your work, your essay will probably need some revision. In the next chapter, you'll learn the specific steps to revising so you can practice them on your own rough drafts.

Chapter 11

From Rough Draft to Finished Product

At last you've gotten your thoughts down on paper and you've written a draft of your essay. Now you're ready to shape and revise it so your essay really says what you want in the most effective way. Although many students feel that the need to rewrite is a sign that they've failed, the truth is that good writing means rewriting. In fact, most professional writers approach their work knowing they'll have to revise it, and they usually write draft after draft until they're satisfied.

To achieve a polished result, you'll need to look at your essay from a variety of angles.

Content

First, you'll want to look at the content of your essay and make sure it:

- actually answers the question posed,

- includes no paragraphs (or parts of paragraphs) that do not contribute to the central idea of your essay, and

- contains all the information your reader needs to understand your point.

Unless your words stick to the topic and contribute directly to your reader's understanding, strike them from your essay. Don't be sidetracked by sentences that simply sound good or raise an interesting point. On the other hand, be sure to add any information that will make your point clearer. Provide background information and details where necessary.

Clarity

With the content of your essay under control, you're ready to focus on clarity. First, check for structure, making sure your reader can easily identify your thesis statement and follow the development of your thoughts through well-placed transitions. Then rephrase any ambiguous statements, even if you believe that your reader will figure out what you're trying to say.

Unlike your teachers at school who may be willing to interpret the ambiguities in your writing because they know and like you, admissions people may not be so generous. They're more likely to assume that you say what you mean. If what you say is unclear, your readers may assume that your thoughts are unclear as well.

Style and Tone

Next, you'll want to turn your attention to your tone and style. Check to see if your essay reflects an appropriate relationship between you and your reader. Then look for and correct any choppy sentences, wordiness, or other stylistic problems that can reduce your reader's understanding and enjoyment of your essay. (For more on this subject, please see chapter 9.)

Correctness

Once you've reworked your essay for content, clarity, style, and tone, you should be on the lookout for errors in spelling, punctuation, and sentence structure. Even the most minor mistake can be distracting. Although your reader may be kind enough to overlook a single error, such as a misplaced comma, he or she may question your writing ability or even your seriousness about applying to college if the errors keep coming. After all, your reader may reason that if you really cared about being admitted, you wouldn't have made all these mistakes.

Proofreading

Once you're satisfied that your essay says what you want in the most effective way, you can make a final copy to submit to the admissions committee. Whether you type or write your final copy, you'll want to make a last check for errors. If you find any, be sure to make your corrections neatly. Unfortunately, a sloppy presentation can turn off your reader as easily as a poorly written essay. If you should botch up the page with crossouts or inserts, seriously consider rewriting your final copy.

Taking your essay from a rough draft to a finished product requires lots of hard work. For those of you wondering how you'll ever be able to stay with your essay long enough to get a great result, you'll be cheered to learn that the more you revise, the easier it becomes.

The checklist below is designed to help you become more confident in your ability to identify weaknesses in your writing. Before you put your application in the mail, you should review this checklist to make sure you're sending off your best effort to the admissions committee.

You've just completed one of the toughest assignments you've probably ever faced. With your applications finished and ready to go, you have a right to feel proud of yourself.

No matter what decision the admissions committee makes, you'll have the satisfaction of knowing that you did the best you could and made the most of the application process.

A CHECKLIST FOR AN EFFECTIVE ESSAY

Content

Your essay:

☐ Answers the question posed.

☐ Makes a significant statement about you.

☐ Demonstrates a match between you and the college.

☐ Includes only information that contributes to your point.

☐ Provides examples and explanations to back up your statements.

Readability

Your essay:

☐ Captures and maintains your reader's attention.

☐ Is well structured

   ☐ Includes both a clear thesis and a preview statement so the reader knows the purpose and direction of your discussion.

   ☐ Includes adequate transitions so your reader can follow your thought process.

☐ Avoids ambiguous statements.

☐ Avoids choppy sentences, passive phrases, wordiness, or other stylistic problems.

Appropriateness

Your essay:

☐ Uses an appropriate tone, such as:

   ☐ friendliness ☐ confidence

   ☐ enthusiasm ☐ respect for authority

☐ Avoids inappropriate tones, such as:

   ☐ groveling ☐ antagonism

   ☐ whining

☐ Shows a respect for your reader's level of understanding:

   ☐ Does not underestimate the reader by belaboring the obvious.

   ☐ Does not assume too much technical knowledge on the reader's part.

Correctness

Your essay:

☐ Provides a neat and attractive format.

☐ Uses acceptable grammar.

☐ Uses proper punctuation.

☐ Uses correct spelling.

Chapter 12

Recycling Your Essays

If you're like most students, you're applying to several colleges. This means you're probably faced with writing several essays. In Chapter 3, you completed a chart to help you keep track of all your essay questions so you'll know how many essays you'll have to write, how long they must be, and, most importantly, how many essays can be recycled for use on more than one application.

In this chapter, you'll be shown some techniques for converting your essays so that you won't have to "recreate the wheel" for every single essay question. In the following pages, you'll be shown how to (1) adapt an essay so that it can be used to answer several different questions, (2) down-size a long essay so that it is suitable for a shorter, more specific essay, and (3) connect several short essays to create a single long one.

ADAPTING AN ESSAY

In some cases, it's obvious that you can substitute one essay for another. When one college, for example, asks you to "describe in detail some special interest, experience, or achievement," you know you can use the same answer to respond to the college that asks you to "evaluate a significant experience or achievement that has special meaning to you." Although the words are slightly different, both colleges want the same information.

Sometimes, however, questions seem so different, so unique, that students are convinced that they'll have to write completely different answers for these questions. Frequently, this is the case—but not always.

In the following examples, you'll see how one student used essentially the same essay to respond to these four strikingly different questions:

1. Write a one-page essay on the following topic: "a conclusion you have reached about a question with no provable answer."

2. You have just completed your 300-page autobiography. Please submit page 217.

3. Describe in detail some special interest, experience, or achievement.

4. Describe a unique aspect of your personality or your experiences. Why is it unique?

It is important to keep in mind that the student who wrote the essays to these questions did not set out at the beginning to find a single unifying approach that would work for all the questions. Rather, the approach evolved as she focused on one question at a time. As she proceeded from question to question, she was able to find some point of commonality or theme that would enable her to adapt the material from the preceding essay to the next. In all cases, you'll notice that in this set of essays, changes were made to the first paragraph only. Once the essay is redirected to respond to the new question, the rest of the essay naturally follows.

Question 1

Write a one-page essay on the following topic: "a conclusion you have reached about a question with no provable answer."

Answer

What makes some people able to transcend their difficulties and lead happy, productive lives? I believe the answer depends on one's outlook. More specifically, if a person is accepting of her deficits rather than dwelling on how they pull her down, she can use her energy to overcome these deficits as well as achieve happiness in other areas.

I have come to the conclusion that no one is dealt a winning hand. Rather, the hand is what a person makes of it. My life, for example, has been filled with hardships. My father died when I was ten, leaving my three-and-a-half-year-old brother and me to grow up with only one parent. To exacerbate an already unfortunate childhood, I developed a serious asthma condition in ninth grade which severely restricted my physical activity and caused me to become more cautious and more anxious about everyday living. Some other person might allow these problems to overwhelm her and make her bitter. She might look around and only see the "lucky ones" who, on the surface, seem to have everything.

I suspect, however, that my friends who have good health and intact families may be wrestling with their own demons, which may not be obvious to others. This insight has helped me to keep my energies focused on solving my problems, rather than on envying someone else. While I certainly hold a bunch of low cards in my hand, my outlook enables me to make the most of my high cards. My sense of humor, for example, allows me to focus on the positive, and my ability to picture my life in the future, having achieved all my dreams, keeps me going strong.

The first question requires the student to think in abstract terms by presenting her perspective on a topic that cannot be proven right or wrong. She uses this question as an opportunity to ponder her optimism in spite of her serious setbacks.

The second question, like the first, is open-ended. It requires the student to write creatively about any aspect of her life for her autobiography. In order for her to use her answer to Question 1 in the second essay, she must find a point of commonality—which she does. In Question 1, she gives the reader a glimpse into her personal philosophy which is certainly an appropriate topic to be included in an autobiography. So, with minor changes to essay one, she writes the following answer to Question 2:

Question 2

You have just completed your 300-page autobiography. Please submit page 217.

Answer

So, I found myself contemplating the answer to this question: What makes some people able to transcend their difficulties and lead happy, productive lives? I believe the answer depends on one's outlook. More specifically, if a person is accepting of her deficits rather than dwelling on how they pull her down, she can use her energy to overcome these deficits as well as achieve happiness in other areas.

I have come to the conclusion that no one is dealt a winning hand. Rather, the hand is what a person makes of it, My life, for example, has been filled with hardships. My father died when I was ten, leaving my three-and-a-half-year-old brother and me to grow up with only one parent. To exacerbate an already unfortunate childhood, I developed a serious asthma condition in ninth grade which severely restricted my physical activity and caused me to become more cautious and more anxious about everyday living. Some other person might allow these problems to overwhelm her and make her bitter. She might look around and only see the "lucky ones" who, on the surface, seem to have everything.

I suspect, however, that my friends who have good health and intact families may be wrestling with their own demons, which may not be obvious to others. This insight has helped me to keep my energies focused on solving my problems, rather than on envying someone else. While I certainly hold a bunch of low cards in my hand, my outlook enables me to make the most of my high cards. My sense of humor, for example, allows me to focus on the positive, and my ability to picture my life in the future, having achieved all my dreams, keeps me going strong.

Question 3 is much more specific than either of the preceding questions. Nevertheless, the student finds a point of commonality. Question 3 asks her to discuss a special interest, experience, or accomplishment. The student reasons that her ability to maintain a positive outlook in spite of her setbacks is, in reality, an accomplishment—perhaps not a conventional accomplishment such as being elected class president but an accomplishment in terms of the goals she has set for herself. By deleting the first paragraph of the preceding essay and by inserting the word "accomplishment" in the second paragraph, she succeeds in answering Question 3.

Question 3
Describe in detail some special interest, experience, or achievement.

Answer
So, I found myself contemplating the answer to this question: What makes some people able to transcend their difficulties and lead happy, productive lives?

I have come to the conclusion that no one is dealt a winning hand. Rather, the hand is what a person makes of it. On the surface, this statement sounds philosophical, but being able to really integrate this concept into the way I live my life has been a significant accomplishment for me.

My life has been filled with hardships. My father died when I was ten, leaving my three-and-a-half-year-old brother and me to grow up with only one parent. To exacerbate an already unfortunate childhood, I developed a serious asthma condition in ninth grade which severely restricted my physical activity and caused me to become more cautious and more anxious about everyday living. Some other person might allow these problems to overwhelm her and make her bitter. She might look around and only see the "lucky ones" who, on the surface, seem to have everything.

I suspect, however, that my friends who have good health and intact families may be wrestling with their own demons, which may not be obvious to others. This insight has helped me to keep my energies focused on solving my problems, rather than on envying someone else. While I certainly hold a bunch of low cards in my hand, my outlook enables me to make the most of my high cards. My sense of humor, for example, allows me to focus on the positive, and my ability to picture my life in the future, having achieved all my dreams, keeps me going strong.

In Question 4, the student is asked to write about either the experience or aspect of her personality that makes her unique. At first glance, Questions 3 and 4 seem worlds apart. After all, what do accomplishments have to do with being unique? The student, however, is able to find another point of commonality, this time by reasoning that her accomplishment is what makes her unique. By finding this connection, she is able to recycle her essay a fourth time!

Question 4

Describe a unique aspect of your personality or your experiences. Why is it unique?

Answer

I have come to the conclusion that no one is dealt a winning hand. Rather, the hand is what a person makes of it. On the surface, this statement sounds philosophical, but being able to really integrate this concept into the way I live my life has been a significant accomplishment for me. is what, I believe, makes me unique.

My life has been filled with hardships. My father died when I was ten, leaving my three-and-a-half-year-old brother and me to grow up with only one parent. To exacerbate an already unfortunate childhood, I developed a serious asthma condition in ninth grade which severely restricted my physical activity and caused me to become more cautious and more anxious about everyday living. Some other person might allow these problems to overwhelm her and make her bitter. She might look around and only see the "lucky ones" who, on the surface, seem to have everything.

I suspect, however, that my friends who have good health and intact families may be wrestling with their own demons, which may not be obvious to others. This insight has helped me to keep my energies focused on solving my problems, rather than on envying someone else. While I certainly hold a bunch of low cards in my hand, my outlook enables me to make the most of my high cards. My sense of humor, for example, allows me to focus on the positive, and my ability to picture my life in the future, having achieved all my dreams, keeps me going strong.

SHORTENING A LONG ESSAY

Frequently you'll find that a long essay written for one application can be used on another application in a shortened version. In the following example, the student wishes to use the same material to answer these two questions:

1. Please write an essay of approximately 500 words on any topic you wish.

2. What extracurricular experience has been most important to you? What do you feel you have accomplished? Please limit your essay to 200 words.

Since the student plans to write about an extracurricular activity in Question 1, he can use the same essay when reduced by 300 words to answer Question 2.

These reductions can be accomplished once the student figures out which information is important to keep and which can be deleted. In general, the way to proceed is to

1. read through the long essay, identifying the points you are trying to make about yourself,

2. determine which sentences state your points and which ones elaborate them, and

3. hang on to the main points at the same time you cut the elaboration. Obviously, the more you cut, the shorter your essay will be.

In the 500-word version below, the student has the luxury of elaborating his important points. The details of his story help to hold his reader's attention. As you read through this essay, notice that the important points have been identified for you in the margins.

> Although I had been a musical director for several shows, the biggest challenge and most rewarding experience of my life was acting as the Musical Director of Hometown Summer Music Theater's (HSMT) production *Hoopla*. The show, a musical comedy by Y.E. Burhar and Ted Fade with music by Tommy Paine and Sheldon Street, was last performed on Broadway in 1950. Burhar wanted to bring it back to Broadway and would be working with HSMT's professional staff and student cast, crew, and orchestra to help him update his show. The script had been revised and five new songs were written.

Important Point

> I was elated. I would not only have responsibility for every musical aspect of the show, but I would also have the chance to work with a famous writer and lyricist. My elation, however, was short lived. I needed (and expected to receive) separate musical parts for fifteen instruments; but all the publisher had was a conductor's score. With only a week to go before auditions, I did not even have a piano part to use at rehearsals.

Important Point

Important Point { I made a cut-and-paste piano score from a photocopy of the handwritten music. It was difficult to read, but it had to suffice. Auditions went well, and the show was cast. Then the tedious job of copying all the instrumental parts began. The first song took two hours to transcribe for one instrument; and with a twenty-song score and fifteen instruments, I began to realize the enormity of the task. I was lucky to find a few charitable souls to help with the copying.

Important Point { *Hoopla* became more than a full-time job. It involved transcribing and arranging music all day and rehearsing until midnight each night. The rehearsals were a welcome change of pace.

I put together a band with little difficulty. But, because the music had to be transcribed, the members could not meet until the third week of rehearsal. Furthermore, since the players were not being paid, they often came late and gave less than their full attention. I found it difficult at first to discipline my peers, but we ultimately worked out that problem.

One unexpected problem was Mr. Burhar. Although he helped the actors, he was nothing but trouble for me when it came to the music. He wanted all of his songs to go at a dirge tempo so that his lyrics would be clear, reminding me of Gilbert's troubles with Sullivan. I, like Sullivan, was unwilling to sacrifice the effectiveness of the music for the lyrics' sake. When dress rehearsals finally started, Burhar began to tell the actors how to perform the music without even bothering to discuss his ideas with me. The members of the cast and band were not willing to put up with it. At our insistence, our director asked the author to leave. That left us only one rehearsal in which to mold the show into shape. That night's work lasted eight hours, but the result was worth the effort.

Important Point { *Hoopla* was a hit! I conducted ten sold-out performances. Standing before the orchestra and cast, I had a feeling of responsibility and intense satisfaction. The applause after each musical number was ample reward for my summer's work. I felt particularly proud to have earned the respect of the 150 people participating in the show and of the entire community.

A quick review of the important points will tell you that the student wants the reader to know that

1. he has musical ability as evidenced by his being musical director for high school shows, but especially for this semi-professional production,

2. he is very serious about his work,

3. he possesses perseverance and leadership qualities, and

4. his production was a success.

In order for the student to get these points across in 200 words, he must eliminate most of the elaboration, as he does below in response to Question 2.

> The biggest challenge and most rewarding experience of my life was acting as the Musical Director of Hometown Summer Music Theatre's (HSMT) production of *Hoopla,* a musical comedy which was last performed on Broadway in 1950. Although I had been a musical director for several shows in high school, it wasn't until this show actually opened that I became aware of just how much I had accomplished.
>
> For this production I had to adapt a single conductor's score into separate musical parts for fifteen instruments. The first song took two hours to transcribe for one instrument; and with a twenty-song score and fifteen instruments, I began to realize the enormity of the task. *Hoopla* became more than a full-time job. It involved transcribing and arranging music all day and rehearsing until midnight each night. With a lot of perseverance, luck, and help from a talented crew and cast, I was able to mold the show into shape. On opening night, standing before the orchestra and cast, I experienced a feeling of intense satisfaction, knowing I had earned the respect of the 150 people participating in the show and of the entire community.

CONNECTING SEVERAL SHORT ESSAYS

After you have worked on a few applications, you may find that you have written several short essays on several different topics. If you're lucky, not only can you reuse these essays to respond to similar questions on other applications, but, sometimes, you can actually connect these answers to make one long essay.

The key to your success is first to find a unifying theme that provides the rationale for combining your shorter essays, and secondly, to develop transitional sentences that will provide the "glue" between each of your shorter essays.

In the following example, the student wrote short essays to respond to these questions:

1. What personal experience has had an impact on you?

2. What paid or volunteer work experience has been most important to you? Why? What do you feel you have accomplished?

3. What extracurricular experience has been most important to you? Why? What do you feel you have accomplished?

When the student was asked on another application to "write a 500-word essay on any topic of genuine interest to you," she decided that all three of her shorter essays could qualify. And, instead of focusing on just one and expanding it, she decided to use all three in their existing forms.

Here are her responses to each of the three short essay questions:

Question 1
What personal experience has had an impact on you?

Answer
Although I am an all-American child, I was born to Israeli parents who have strong ties to Israel. My extended family provides an interesting counterpoint to my American experience. For example, I have cousins living in Israel, roughly the same age as I, who will be entering the Israeli army at the same time I will be entering college. They must join the army for at least three years; if they refuse to make this commitment, they are exiled from the country. While college is something that requires a lot of responsibility, it in no way compares with the commitment that Israeli teenagers make to their country. Furthermore, Israeli youth are extremely concerned with local and world affairs because these affairs both directly and indirectly affect their lives. The average American youth does not know much about current events. However, I am more aware than most of my friends of international, national, and political concerns. My extended family has helped me to realize how important it is to be connected to the world and not be egocentric.

Question 2

What paid or volunteer work experience has been most important to you? Why? What do you feel you have accomplished?

Answer

The fact that volunteering to play piano and spend time at the Beth Israel Nursing Home is most important to me is extremely ironic. A year ago, I would have shied away from old people, but today I look forward to spending time with the elderly. Why was I afraid of old people? Through the years, I had been misguided by the idea that old people are not really people; they were just old. Since all of my grandparents lived in Israel, I was deprived of the opportunity for a relationship with an old person. What did old people have to to share with me? A year ago, I could not have answered this question. But through my work at Beth Israel, I was able to overcome my fear and recognize the knowledge and wisdom old people have to offer.

It seems odd, given my fear of old people, that I would devote a sizable portion of my free time to playing classical music for them on the piano on weekends. Having studied for eleven years, I knew I could perform the pieces well.

When I first started my work, I was scared. But after I finished my concert, I was overwhelmed by the response. These people suddenly opened up and enthusiastically drowned me in their stories. People whom I thought were incapable of speaking could not stop talking. Almost immediately, I lost my fear of these people. They were nothing to be scared of at all. In fact, I enjoyed talking with them. I realized how foolish I was for having shied away from old people for so long. Old people are really people, with feelings and emotions. What did old people have to share with me? A lifetime.

Question 3

What extracurricular experience has been most important to you? Why? What do you feel you have accomplished?

Answer

The position of Chief Catalog Editor of the yearbook is the extracurricular activity which is most important to me. In this capacity I insure that students actually sit for their pictures, match up faces with names and alphabetize them. I also type all the copy and prepare an intricate index which lists the names of 1500 students and cross references them with their pictures which can appear anywhere in the 300-page text. Clearly, this is not a glamorous job. It requires a great deal of time and patience.

Despite the drudgery, I really love this work. What keeps me going is knowing that in June, when the yearbooks are distributed, students will have a complete and accurate record of the year's events. While most students will not even stop to think about how their picture and name managed to appear correctly in the yearbook, I will have the personal satisfaction of knowing that I have had such a strong impact on a tangible memory which students will treasure for the rest of their lives.

In order to connect all three of these very different essays, the student found a concept that could unify them: conveying the essence of her diverse personality. Having found a unifying theme, she could then focus on creating transitional sentences between each short essay. Obviously, the better the transitional sentences, the more seamless will be the effect of the larger essay.

The following 500-word essay is the result of some hard work. Notice the sentences she deletes from the original versions and the ones she adds, especially the transitions which are marked in the margins. Also, look at how she restates her theme in the concluding paragraph to firmly hold the whole essay together.

Question 4

Write a 500-word essay on any topic of genuine interest to you.

Answer

I am about to complete a task I never thought possible. In a 500-word essay, I am preparing to reveal the essence of myself: complex, sensitive, fun-loving, hard-working—and modest!   } *Theme*

Although I am an all-American child, I was born to Israeli parents who have strong ties to Israel. My extended family provides an interesting counterpoint to my American experience. For example, I have cousins living in Israel, roughly the same age as I, who will be entering the Israeli army at the same time I will be entering college. They must join the army for at least three years; if they refuse to make this commitment, they are exiled from the country. While college is something that requires a lot of responsibility, it in no way compares with the commitment that Israeli teenagers make to their country. Furthermore, Israeli youth are extremely concerned with local and world affairs because these affairs both directly and indirectly affect their lives. The average American youth does not know much about current events. However, I am more aware than most of my friends of international, national, and political concerns. My extended family has helped me to realize how important it is to be connected to the world and not be egocentric. They have also helped me to extend myself to help others. Accordingly, I have volunteered to play the piano for the elderly at the Beth Israel Nursing Home.   } *Transition*

The fact that volunteering to play piano and spend time at the Beth Israel Nursing Home is most important to me is extremely ironic. A year ago, I would have shied away from old people, but today I look forward to spending time with the elderly. Why was I afraid of old people? Through the years, I had been misguided by the idea that old people are not really people; they were just old. Since all of my grandparents lived in Israel, I was deprived of the opportunity for a relationship with an old person. What did old people have to share with me? A year ago, I could not have answered this question. But through my work at Beth Israel, I was able to overcome my fear and recognize the knowledge and wisdom old people have to offer.

It seems odd, given my fear of old people, that I would devote a sizable portion of my free time to playing classical music for them on the piano on weekends. Having studied for eleven years, I knew I could perform the pieces well.

When I first started my work, I was scared. But after I finished my concert, I was overwhelmed by the response. These people suddenly opened up and enthusiastically drowned me in their stories. People whom I thought were incapable of speaking could not stop talking. Almost immediately, I lost my fear of these people. They were nothing to be scared of at all. In fact, I enjoyed talking with them. I realized how foolish I was for having shied away from old people for so long. Old people are really people, with feelings and emotions. What did old people have to share with me? A lifetime.

Transition {
As much as I enjoy giving my energy to people who are entering the final stages of life, I am also devoted to my peers. As Chief Catalog Editor, I make a significant contribution to the yearbook, which provides a tangible memory of our high school years. The position of Chief Catalog Editor of the yearbook is the extracurricular activity which is most important to me. In this capacity I insure that students actually sit for their pictures, match up faces with names and alphabetize them. I also type all the copy and prepare an intricate index which lists the names of 1500 students and cross references them with their pictures which can appear anywhere in the 300-page text. Clearly, this is not a glamorous job. It requires a great deal of time and patience.

Despite the drudgery, I really love this work. What keeps me going is knowing that in June, when the yearbooks are distributed, students will have a complete and accurate record of the year's events. While most students will not even stop to think about how their picture and name managed to appear correctly in the yearbook, I will have the personal satisfaction of knowing that I have had such a strong impact on a tangible memory which students will treasure for the rest of their lives.

Theme {
While I have been able to present some essential aspects of myself in this essay, the only way to get to know the real me is to watch me in action as a matriculating student at ABC University.

Knowing you can reuse your essays for more than one application and knowing the techniques for recycling them can give you added confidence as you work through this book and write your college applications.

Chapter 13

Applying Electronically

The electronic revolution has arrived on the college application scene! Colleges are taking advantage of technology to put their applications on the Internet in an effort to make filling them out easier for you and to help admissions officers reach as many students as possible.

If you choose to apply electronically, you will be faced with a variety of products (some developed by the colleges themselves, others by software companies under contract to the colleges) and a variety of procedures for completing the electronic admissions process.

If after reading this section, you decide that electronic admissions will make life easier for you, and you are feeling ready for a bit of an adventure, then you should feel free to pursue this option.

However, if

—the process makes you feel anxious, or

—you or your high school do not have access to computer facilities and software, or

—you just feel more secure using your word processor, typewriter, or ball point pen,

then

you should feel free to apply to college in the traditional way, without giving a thought to your friends or family who may be using or encouraging you to use the new technology.

You'll be better able to maintain your sanity if you can keep firmly in mind what admissions officers across the country are saying:

1. There *is no admissions advantage* to using electronic applications instead of paper ones.

2. When it comes to applying to college, a pen and neat handwriting will never become obsolete.

3. Although computer access may appear to be everywhere, a significant portion of students across the country do not have ready access to computers at home, in school, or in their communities. Until all of the major "players"—the colleges, the high schools, and the applicants—have equal access to computer technology and feel comfortable with it, the paper application, filled out manually and sent by U.S. Mail, will remain the primary method of applying to college.

Keeping these trends in mind, the goal of this chapter is to inform you of the types of electronic services that are available for your use and to provide you with a procedure that will enable you to apply to college electronically with ease.

APPLYING VIA THE INTERNET

In the recent past, colleges provided different ways of applying electronically using floppy disks, CD-ROMs, and the Internet. However, as the Internet has emerged as the primary source of information, colleges are increasingly offering their applications on their own home pages and on other well-traveled sites as well. The level of sophistication at each school's Web site varies with the school's resources, personality, and philosophy and ranges from enabling a student to:

- view the application and print it out, so it can be hand or typewritten and mailed to the college;

- download the application to the student's computer, type information directly on the application, and print out the completed application to be mailed to the college; or

- fill in the application on the computer and electronically send the completed application directly to the college. (No stamps, no envelopes, no checks required—just a credit card!)

By creating a customized home page where a student can learn about the school's academic programs and college life, as well as admissions and scholarship information, the college can creatively express itself and distinguish itself from other schools. Colleges like displaying information on their home pages because they can control the content and format, and they can also keep the home pages up to date. Since use of the home page is free to any student who has access to the Internet, colleges know that being on the Net can increase their chances of being "visited" by curious students, who may eventually become real applicants.

About the Home Page

At a home page site, you will usually find a greeting and a list of what information is available. When you point to any highlighted item and you click on it, you are immediately transported there. Although college home pages may vary in style and content, they usually include information on academics, athletics, campus life, student activities, residential life, scholarship and financial aid, and admissions information.

One of the beauties of the Net is that you can download sections of the home page, including the application, onto your own system. From there, you can interact with the information and make requests that you can send directly to the college.

Getting to a College Home Page

You can arrive at most colleges' home pages by typing

www.(name or initials of college).edu

If you are not sure of the name or initials a particular college uses, you can get the address at

www.utexas.edu/world/univ/state/

This address will bring you to a site that lists every college's home page, alphabetically or geographically.

Finding the Common Application

The National Association of Secondary School Principals (NASSP) is the organization responsible for developing and distributing the Common Application. You can receive the Common Application at the following addresses:

www.nassp.org

or

www.commonap.org

The Internet version of the Common Application, which you can download onto your own computer, is the same as the paper, version, which you can receive from your counselor. The advantage to using the online version is that you can type your responses directly onto the application, print it out, and download any supplementary forms specifically required by your colleges as well.

The NASSP also makes a disk version of the Common Application, available in both Windows and Mac. A copy of each version is available to your counselor at no charge and may be copied.

For more information about the Common Application, please refer back to Chapter 2.

Finding Scholarships

If you are looking for a scholarship, the following address will take you to a site where you can conduct a scholarship search for colleges across the United States:

www.fastweb.com

This site provides a customized search of more than 180,000 private scholarships, fellowships, grants, and loans. All you have to do is input your demographics and indicate your areas of interest, and, in about 15 minutes, Fastweb will provide you with the results of your search. To keep the scholarship service free, Fastweb has attracted corporate sponsors, such as American Express, that want to reach college and graduate students.

Online Registration for SAT I and SAT II

www.collegeboard.com

This site connects you directly to the College Board, which among other activities, administers the SAT I and SAT II. Once here, you will be offered an array of services, including online registration for the SAT I and SAT II, a calendar of test dates for the academic year, a schedule of fees, and a limited college search engine that can help you select a list of appropriate schools to which you can apply. (Please see the discussion of ExPAN on page 128.)

Information on College and Career

www.petersons.com

Peterson's provides information about hundreds of colleges and universities, as well as information about study abroad, career and jobs, summer programs, and more. Peterson's online services are designed to help reduce the stress of selecting colleges and applying to them. Students who click onto BestCollegePicks (www.bestcollegepicks.com) can discover the colleges that can best meet their career, income, and lifestyle goals. In addition, students can apply to colleges using the Common Application, which is available at the Peterson's Web site.

How to Find Web Sites Not Listed Here

*E*very day, new Web sites appear on the Internet, which means that the Web sites listed here are by no means complete. In fact, you may find some new and interesting sites on your own by conducting your own search. The addresses of four useful search engines are listed below:

www.webcrawler.com

www.yahoo.com

www.altavista.com/

www.google.com/

Once you have gained access to any of these search engines, you can begin to look for sites on college admissions, as well as on a multitude of other topics. Here are some typical phrases you might want to use in your search. Of course, you can always make up some of your own. (Be sure to keep phrases in quotation marks or each word will be searched separately!)

"Admissions Offices" "American Universities"

"Financial Aid" "College Applications"

"Colleges and Universities" "Common Application"

Finding Products and Services on the Net

To find a list of Web sites offering services and products for college admissions, simply go to your favorite search engine (e.g., Yahoo, Google) and search for "companies and admissions." Here, you will be provided with a list of vendors who are selling information, products, and services that they believe will help you as you apply to college. Be aware that anyone can create a home page to advertise his or her wares. As a result, if you have not seen the product or service before, you have no way of knowing the quality of what you may be buying.

Also, don't forget that you will be *billed* for whatever you order. So be sure to check with your parents before you buy.

Free Services

In response to students' enthusiasm for computer technology in education, various nonprofit agencies and for-profit companies have launched new products and services at no cost to students. Here is a helpful service that is expected to maintain a consistent presence over the next several years and is free to the students who use it.

ExPAN: Guidance and Application Network

ExPAN is a product, created and distributed by the College Board, which is designed to streamline the college admission process by connecting students, high schools, and colleges electronically through an interactive information network.

If your high school is part of the network, you can use ExPAN to receive valuable information. More specifically, ExPAN can equip you with the ability to search an extensive college and scholarship database to provide lists of colleges that match your specific academic and social needs. You can also determine your actual college contribution through the use of a computerized financial aid worksheet. The ExPAN network is paid for by the high schools and colleges, so there is no cost to you. If, however, you should decide to use ExPAN to apply to colleges, you will be charged a fee per school. So, to save money, it's best to apply on line at the school's home page or with the Common Application.

The only place you can access the ExPAN network is at a designated workstation in your high school. This means that you will have to share the workstation and its resources with other students.

HOW TO PROCEED

To help you proceed with filling out your application, using any of the electronic devices or services, you should go directly to the college's Web page. Here, you can find answers to the following questions:

1. Does the college provide its application on the Internet?

2. Does the college accept the Common Application? If so, does it require you to fill out a supplemental form?

3. Does the college want the completed application submitted in paper form and sent through the U.S. Mail or submitted electronically?

If you can't find the answers to these or other questions you may have, you can always call the admissions office directly. The people who work there will be able to tell you of any particular requirements for their college.

TIPS AND REMINDERS

Tips

- If you choose to apply using the Internet, be sure to give yourself enough time to both find and reach your destination. Under ideal circumstances, you should be able to find and connect to the Web site of your choice easily and quickly. But, with new technology, many an unexpected "glitch" can get in your way. For example, you may find there are so many people using the Internet when you are that your browser may operate very slowly and, in some cases, it may not be allowed to access the sites you want because of their overuse. If you wait until the last minute to start your applications over the Internet, you may find that you have run out of time.

- Be sure to keep your counselor in the information loop. With so much information floating around on the Internet and with so much opportunity for you to search and make decisions independently, it can be easy for you to forget to check in with your counselor. Your counselor can save you a lot of time and trouble. He or she not only knows you and the colleges to which you are thinking of applying but also knows what your chances are of getting into those schools. If you apply electronically without first consulting your counselor, he or she may not be able to advise you until after the fact.

- In order to complete your application, you will need to give your teachers and guidance counselors a hard (paper) copy of the appropriate recommendation and transcript forms to fill out. Do not forget to print out these pages so you can distribute them to your teachers and counselor in a timely fashion.

Reminders

- There is *no admissions advantage* to using electronic applications instead of paper ones.

- Colleges will always accept an application that is neatly handwritten in ink.

- Be careful when you purchase goods and services over the Internet. Remember: There is no free lunch; you will be expected to pay for whatever you order, and the only way to judge the quality of the goods and services offered over the Internet is to buy them. So, buyer beware!

- If you are in doubt about anything concerning admissions, call the college admissions office and see your counselor.

Appendix *A*

An Analysis of Three Good Essays

Throughout *College Applications and Essays*, you've read several parts of essays selected to illustrate a variety of specific writing points. In this section, you'll not only have an opportunity to read through three essays in their entirety, but you'll also be treated to analyses that examine the essays for their overall effectiveness.

ESSAY I

QUESTION

Please write on a topic of your choice.

ANSWER

I've often asked myself what is it about tennis that attracts me to it that goes beyond hitting the ball over the net, demanding so much of my free time? When I first started to play in tennis tournaments, I would play my match, win or lose, and go home. But soon these tournaments and matches became a way of life for me. Tennis has helped to increase my awareness of the different personalities that I encounter. Through the lens of the tennis court, I've learned a great deal about other people as well as myself. I've learned about the human qualities I respect by seeing them emerge in the course of a tennis match and especially what happens before and after a match.

A quality that I really value in one of my tennis friends, Sandra, is her positive attitude. If someone tells her that her tennis game is great because she has exceptional agility, but that she needs work on her groundstrokes, she focuses only on the positive. She walks away more confident than she was before. Rather than dwelling on the fact that she needs to work on her groundstrokes, she focuses on the fact that someone has complimented her on her agility and athleticism. I remember when I first began to play tennis competitively that I tended to focus on the negative comments. So, if my coach told me that my footwork needed improvement, but my groundstrokes were very good, I would dwell on my weakness to the point that I'd forget about my strengths. Sometimes I imagined my feet were immersed in glue. Others times I felt like I had ten-pound weights attached to my ankles. During that time, I rarely thought about the strengths of my strokes; my feet got all the attention. However, from knowing Sandra and how she always saw the glass as half full rather than half-empty, I have become more positive about myself. Now, I am more likely to act on the positive and even find the positive in seemingly bleak situations.

In addition to Sandra's positive attitude, I also admire her fearless nature. Before she plays her match, she never checks the draw sheet to see whom her opponent is. Instead, she goes out on the court like it is her duty to win, no matter who she is playing. Since she never shows any intimidation, other players fear her. Following Sandra's example, I go out on the court, looking confident as I can, although inside I may feel less certain. I've adopted the motto: "Fake it till you make it."

While Sandra approaches tennis with a no-nonsense, positive attitude, my friend Judy exudes a more modest style that I also greatly admire. Even though Judy has great technique, her strength is in her poise and maturity, which enables her to "comeback" after she's down a set. When she's losing, she does not panic or become sullen. Rather, she maintains her composure. Similarly, when she's winning, she doesn't give in to her excitement. Instead, she keeps her goals steadily in mind. Over the years of playing with Judy and watching her play others, I have become inspired by her example. Whenever I begin to feel frazzled, I picture her poise and maturity in my mind, and I feel transformed. I admire her steady determination, and I try to model myself after her.

Tennis is a game where it is easy to forget that one's opponent is a person, but Judy always approaches her opponent with deep respect. This is another quality that I admire in her and am cultivating in myself. When my opponent slides and falls, for example, my first reaction is to worry about her rather than to enjoy the advantage I may have gained at her expense. I have learned that the well being of the player is more important than simply winning.

What I've discovered over the years of playing tennis is that tennis not only develops skill, but it also develops character. While I love the physical aspects of the game, I am even more attracted to the personal qualities that players bring to it. In a tennis match, the human experience can be played out in miniature. Fear and confidence, strength and weakness, ego and humility all play a role. In tennis, the spectrum of human qualities is on display and each player can decide which ones to take on. My friends and opponents inspire me to become the best person I can possibly be. No wonder I love this game so much.

ANALYSIS OF ESSAY 1
STRATEGY AND CONTENT
Since most of this student's time and energy is channeled into playing tennis, she writes this essay to show that she is more than just an athlete. By reflecting on qualities she admires in her teammates and then relating those qualities back to herself, she gives the admissions committee an insight into what she values, who she is, and whom she hopes to become.

READABILITY
The writer grabs the reader's attention by leading off with a question that the reader would like answered. She clearly states the central idea at the end of the first paragraph ("I've learned about human qualities that I respect by seeing them emerge during the course of a tennis match. . . ."), and she develops this idea by describing qualities of a different teammate in each succeeding paragraph. The final paragraph focuses the reader back on the student and reveals aspects of the student's personality about which the admissions committee would like to know.

APPROPRIATENESS
Since the writer is an excellent tennis player, it would be easy for her to boast about her accomplishments. Fortunately, the writer avoids this trap by writing with humility toward her topic and respect toward the admissions committee. She accomplishes these tones by both downplaying her skills and by admiring the skills of her teammates.

CORRECTNESS
This essay uses correct grammar, punctuation, and spelling.

ESSAY II

QUESTION

Please write a brief essay on any subject you choose. We would like to know anything of interest to you that will help us better understand you.

ANSWER

Adults tend to label adolescence as a difficult stage in development, but adults often have trouble knowing just how to help teenagers with their problems. Some of my friends realized that we were the ones best suited to helping one another with our growing pains. We would sit informally and discuss problems that seemed monstrous to us, but when we analyzed them we discovered that they were not so unusual or upsetting. Based on this realization, we decided to formalize our discussions and open a peer-counseling center where any student could come to discuss any problem. My experience in peer counseling has helped me to mature and develop new interpersonal skills, and I have gained confidence in my ability to handle my problems more successfully in the future.

When I first became involved in peer counseling, I was the one receiving help. When my brother, John, informed me and my parents that he was not going to attend college, I felt an increased burden to achieve to compensate for my brother's lack of motivation. As a result, I became depressed. I discussed my problem with other students in the peer-counseling center and realized that I was placing an unnecessary burden on myself because, in reality, my parents never asked me to work harder. I simply felt guilty about my brother's decision and that caused my depression.

By working through this problem, I realized the value of sharing my concerns and decided to help other students feel better about themselves. When my friend told me about the problems she had at home with her mother and her stepfather, I asked her to come to the center. At first she was reluctant to reveal herself because she was afraid others would not understand, but her need to share was more compelling. The example of my own success helped me to persuade my friend that by discussing her problems, she could deal with her situation at home more effectively and also feel better about herself. As one of her peer counselors, I was able to understand her needs. As a result, I could help her formulate a plan of action to overcome her difficulties.

I know that the experience I have gained through peer counseling will be of use to me in whatever career I pursue. The ability to listen, analyze, and develop a plan of action is essential to everyday problem solving. I am confident that when I go away to school I will be able to deal with my problems and share my strength with others.

ANALYSIS OF ESSAY II
STRATEGY AND CONTENT

In this essay, the student focuses on her emotional growth, and by sharing some personal feelings and experiences with the admissions people, she is able to get them to take a special interest in her. The fact that the essay initially exposes some of her minor weaknesses is effectively countered by the student's ability to demonstrate at the end of the essay her growth and strength. The two examples she uses—one that tells how peer counseling helped her and another that tells how she was able to use peer counseling to help someone else—let the reader see the stages of her personal development.

READABILITY

The essay opens with an attention getter—a statement about adult/adolescent behavior—and continues to keep the reader's interest by providing ingenuous revelations and concrete examples. The structure also helps the reader along. Starting with some essential background information, the first paragraph works its way toward a clear thesis statement that provides the direction for the essay. The following paragraphs develop the thesis, leading to a strong conclusion that provides a glimpse into the writer's future. The writing style enhances the reader's experience. The sentences are active, vigorous, and to the point. Well-placed transitions allow the writer to move from point to point effortlessly.

APPROPRIATENESS

The essay expresses an appropriate reader-writer relationship. From her tone, the writer seems to be at once vulnerable yet confident, friendly yet respectful of authority.

CORRECTNESS

The essay uses correct grammar, punctuation, and spelling.

ESSAY III

QUESTION

Evaluate a significant experience, achievement, or risk that you have taken and it's impact on you.

ANSWER

Tom Zincer succeeded in his task. My science class's first field trip took place on a bitter cold February day in Maine. Tom, our science teacher, led the group of relatively puzzled, well-bundled students into the forest. I was right behind Tom, and the sound of his red boots breaking through the thin layer of ice that covered the crusty snow seemed to bounce off the trees and scare away the few singing birds that had not migrated south for the winter. We stopped fourteen times during that four-hour field trip to hear Tom ramble on about the bark of "this" deciduous tree and the habitat that "this" coniferous tree need to grow. We examined animal droppings and tracks in the snow and traced a bird's song back to its singer. This was all meaningless to me. I was cold and bored and wanted the field trip to end.

I would later write several essays in my journal about the fact that writing a detailed seven-page analysis of the field trip took all the beauty out of the event. I would complain to Tom about how boring and mundane his class was and how impossible it was to be so "anally" observant. I argued that no field trip could ever be enjoyable if we had to write down and later analyze the percentage of deciduous and coniferous trees, the air temperature, the amount of snow on the ground, the slope of the course taken, the change in temperature over the day, and a plethora of other minutia. Basically, I was lazy. No, no. I was not lazy. I was just not ready; I was not yet ready to become an observer.

"Sam, just trust me on this one. You'll thank me later," Tom said at the conclusion of our meeting. I had gone to see Tom privately in order to discuss how I could survive his class. The minutia was killing me, and my slow death was reflected in my dismal grade. Upon leaving that meeting, I made a personal and academic decision to develop my observational skills, both to please my teacher and to avoid the disappointment of another "D+."

On my next field trip, I set out into the forest with two pencils cocked between my two ears like guns ready to fire. My teeth were clenched with the determination to stay focused throughout the entire field trip and write down every word that man uttered. However, I constantly felt myself drifting, and while my mind wandered, the group advanced significantly ahead of me, and I missed the sighting of another bird. I ran up to the group just in time to hear Tom start his lecture about a nearby rock formation. Instead of listening, I was asking my friend to see his Picasso-like rendition of the bird. I, therefore, fell behind on the lecture, and so went the endless cycle: fall behind, try to catch up, fall more behind. When it came time to rewrite my field notes in legible form, I stared at a piece of paper that consisted of smudged squiggly lines and eventually tears. Frustrated and disappointed, I retreated back to my cabin to seek refuge.

I quickly got undressed and slipped under my blanket for warmth, comfort, and most importantly protection. After I gave myself a few minutes to calm down, I took out the wet crumbled piece of paper from my pocket and tried to redraw a stick figure of a bird. The twelve stick figures, representing the twelve different birds we saw, looked exactly the same, and trying to redraw each body part of each bird to scale was so difficult that I felt like each pen stroke was met with a ton of resistance. Giving up, I pushed the piece of paper back into my pocket and lay down on my back. I saw Simon sitting in his characteristically feminine position on Ethan's bed. Simon was sitting, facing Ethan, with his legs crossed and his right hand casually nestled on his right kneecap, his foot twitching like the tail of a happy dog. Ethan was lying on his side with his big black headphones cupped around his ears, reading Faulkner. As my head swiveled, I noticed Conrad, sleeping, as usual, with his blanket clenched tightly under his chin, with both fists. I heard Fred and Rob discussing the pitfalls of modern education and could see Donald's head rhythmically moving back and forth, in sync with Jimmy Hendrix. I then realized that I too was part of my environment. I realized that I was a silent participant, and more importantly, I realized that I was an observer.

On my next field trip, I had one pencil nonchalantly nestled on top of my right ear. I set out with no mission in mind and had no vengeance in my heart. I intentionally lagged behind my fellow classmates in order to get a wider, broader perspective of the environment. Applying what I learned in my cabin, I was able to engage all of my senses and could attempt to take in the vastness of it all. When we returned from our field trip, the task of doing a "rewrite" did not seem so odious, and my pencil flew across the page like a writer who just experienced an epiphany and wants to get his idea down before he forgets it. I drew every bird, tree, and rock as best I could, and although they were not perfect, they were exactly what I saw.

ANALYSIS OF ESSAY III

STRATEGY AND CONTENT

In this essay, the student intends to show how he grew both emotionally and academically. In the beginning, he believes so strongly that his field trips are worthless that he actually tries to persuade his teacher of his point of view. The student then takes the reader along on his "journey" from resistance and self-doubt to the discovery that he can do what the teacher requires of him. This essay is particularly successful because the reader can really see the student's struggle and ultimate triumph.

READABILITY

This essay grabs the reader's attention right away and succeeds in keeping it. The first sentence, "Tom Zincer succeeded in his task" raises the question in the reader's mind: who is Tom Zincer, and what was his task? The question is immediately answered, and, through the use of vivid storytelling in which the story is developed chronologically, the reader experiences the student's journey from "non observer" to "observer." In addition, the thesis is clearly stated at the end of the second paragraph: "Basically, I was lazy. No. No. I was not lazy. I was just not ready; I was not yet ready to become an observer." In the rest of the essay, the writer shows how he becomes an "observer."

APPROPRIATENESS

The tone of this essay is effective because it relies on humor and a dose of self-deprecation to makes its point. In addition, the writer describes his feelings, his situation, and his surroundings so vividly and in such a personal way that the reader can almost see the wheels of the student's mind turn as he writes.

CORRECTNESS

This essay uses proper grammar, punctuation, and spelling.

A Sample Application

In this section, you will see the student's parts of the Common Application filled in by computer. You will also see a sample essay. You'll also notice that the secondary school report form, the recommendation form, and the financial aid application are not included here.

2000-2001 Common Application ©

Application for Undergraduate Admission

Member colleges and universities encourage the use of this application. No distinction will be made between it and the college's own form. The accompanying instructions tell you how to complete, copy, and file your application with any one or several of the colleges.

Personal Data   ☒ **Male**

Legal Name: Beck _____   Ronald _____   _____   _____   ☐ **Female**
                  Last/Family   First   Middle (complete)   Jr., etc.

Prefer to be called: Ronny _____ (nickname)   **Former last name(s) if any:** _____

Applying as a   ☒ **Freshman**   ☐ **Transfer**   **For the term beginning:**   Fall, 2001 _____

Permanent home address: 15 Oak Ave. _____
                              Number and Street

Hometown _____   NY ____   USA _____   12345-6789 _____
City or Town   State   Country   Zip Code + 4 or Postal Code

Is your mailing address for admissions correspondence the same?   ☒ **Yes**

Mailing address: 15 Oak Ave. _____   **Use from:** _____   **To:** _____
                       Number and Street

Hometown _____   NY ____   USA _____   12345-6789 _____
City or Town   State   Country   Zip Code + 4 or Postal Code

Phone at mailing address: _____   **Phone at permanent address:** 999-123-4567 _____
                          Include area code   Include area code

E-mail address: Ron.Beck@School.com _____

Birthdate (mm/dd/yy): 05/18/83   **Citizenship:** ☒ **U.S./dual U.S. citizen.**   **If dual, specify other citizenship:** _____

☐ **U.S. Permanent resident visa.**   **Citizen of:** _____   ☐ **Other citizenship.**   **Please specify country:** _____

If you are not a U.S. citizen and live in the United States, how long have you been in the country? _____ **Visa Type:** _____

Possible area(s) of academic concentration/major: History; Pre-Law _____   ☐ **Or undecided**

Special college or division if applicable: _____

Possible career or professional plans: Business; Law _____   ☐ **Or undecided**

Will you be a candidate for financial aid?   ☐ **Yes**   ☒ **No**   **If yes, the appropriate form(s) was/will be filed on (mm/dd/yy):** _____

The following items are optional. No information you provide will be used in a discriminatory manner.

Social Security number, if any: 123-45-6789 _____   **Marital status:** Single _____

Place of birth: Hometown _____   NY ____   USA _____
                      City or Town   State   Country

First language, if other than English: _____   **Language spoken at home:** English _____

If you wish to be identified with a particular ethnic group, please check all that apply:

☐ **African American, Black**   ☐ **Mexican American, Chicano**

☐ **Native American, Alaskan Native**   (Tribal affiliation _____   Enrolled _____)   ☐ **Native Hawaiian, Pacific Islander**

☐ **Asian American**   (Country of family's origin _____)   (mm/yy)   ☐ **Puerto Rican**

☐ **Asian, including Indian Subcontinent**   (Country _____)   ☒ **White or Caucasian**

☐ **Hispanic, Latino**   (Country _____)   ☐ **Other**   (Specify _____)

2000-2001   **Ronald Beck** _____   123-45-6789 _____   APP-1

Educational Data

School you now attend: Hometown High School

Date of Entry (mm/yy): 09/97

Address: Hometown   NY   12345-6789

CEEB/ACT code: 12321

Date of secondary graduation (mm/yy): 06/01   **School is** ☒ Public ☐ Private ☐ Parochial

College counselor: Name: Ms. Jane Revere   **Position:** Guidance Counselor

Counselor's phone: 333-123-4567   **ext:** _____   **Counselor's fax:** 333-123-4568

List all other secondary schools, including summer schools and programs you have attended beginning with ninth grade.

Name of School	Location (City, State, Zip)	Dates Attended	
Hometown HS	Hometown, NY, 12345-6789	09/97	06/01

List all colleges at which you have taken courses for credit and list names of courses taken and grades earned on a separate sheet. Please have an official transcript sent from each institution as soon as possible.

Name of College	Location (City, State, Zip)	Degree Candidate?	Dates Attended
		☐	
		☐	
		☐	

☐ If not currently attending school, please check here.   Describe in detail, on a separate sheet, your activities since last enrolled.

Test Information

Be sure to note the tests required for each institution to which you are applying. The official scores from the appropriate testing agency must be submitted to each institution as soon as possible. Please list your test plans below.

ACT   Date Taken/ to be taken   Date

mm/yy	English Score	Math Score	Reading Score	Science Score	Composite Score

SAT I   Date Taken/ to be taken

mm/yy	English Score	Math Score	Reading Score	Science Score	Composite Score
05/99	560	690			

SAT II Subject Tests   Date

mm/yy	Verbal	Math		mm/yy	Verbal	Math
05/98	Biology	610		05/00	Writing	570
mm/yy	Subject	Score		mm/yy	Subject	Score
05/99	MathII	670				
mm/yy	Subject	Score		mm/yy	Subject	Score
mm/yy	Subject	Score		mm/yy	Subject	Score

Test of English as a second language (TOEFL or other exam)   Date Taken/ to be taken

mm/yy	Subject	Score		mm/yy	Subject	Score
mm/yy	Test	Score		mm/yy	Test	Score

Family

Mother's full name: Susan Beck

Is she living? Yes

Home address if different from yours:

Father's full name: Thomas V. Beck

Is he living? Yes

Home address if different from yours:

Occupation (describe briefly): Teacher/Writer

Name of business or organization: _____

College (if any): Syracuse University

Degree: B.S.   **Year:** 1971

Professional or graduate school (if any): Columbia U.

Degree: MBA   **Year:** 1977

Occupation (describe briefly): Real Estate

Name of business or organization: Wicky Real Estate

College (if any): Lake Forest College

Degree: B.A.   **Year:** 1970

Professional or graduate school (if any): Columbia U.

Degree: MBA   **Year:** 1976

If not with both parents, with whom do you make your permanent home:

Please check if parents are ☒ Married ☐ Separated ☐ Divorced **Date:** _____ ☐ Other

2000-2001   Ronald Beck   123-45-6789   APP-2

Please give names and ages of your brothers or sisters. If they have attended college, give the names of the institutions attended, degrees, and approximate dates:
Gwen,21, Lehigh University, B.A., 2001

Academic Honors

Briefly describe any scholastic distinctions or honors you have won beginning with ninth grade:

I received an award for excellence in Spanish in 10th grade.

Extracurricular, Personal, and Volunteer Activities (including summer)

Please list your principal extracurricular, community, and family activities and hobbies in the order of their interest to you. Include specific events and/or major accomplishments such as musical instruments played, varsity letters earned, etc. Please mark in the right column those activities you hope to pursue in college. To allow us to focus on the highlights of your activities, please complete this section even if you plan to attach a resume.

| Activity | Grade level or post-secondary (p.s.) | | | | | Approximate time spent | | Positions held, honors won, or letters earned | Do you plan to participate in college? |
	9	10	11	12	PS	Hours per week	Weeks per year		
Tae Kwan Do	☒	☒	☒	☒	☐	12-15	40	Black Belt,Instruct	☒
Drama Club	☒	☒	☐	☐	☐	5-10	15		☒
Lacrosse	☐	☒	☒	☒	☐	12-15	15		☐
Safe Rides	☐	☐	☒	☒	☐	3	40		☐
	☐	☐	☐	☐	☐				☐
	☐	☐	☐	☐	☐				☐
	☐	☐	☐	☐	☐				☐

Work Experience

List any job (including summer employment) you have held during the past three years.

Specific nature of work	Employer	Approximate dates of employment From	To	Approximate no. of hours per week
Tae Kwan Do Instructor	Tigerman's Tae Kwan Do	09/00	06/01	9
Camp Counselor	Camp Redwood	06/01	08/01	40
Drama Teacher	Hometown Kids Drama Grou	06/00	08/00	40

In the space provided below or on a separate sheet if necessary, please describe which of these activities (extracurricular and personal activities or work experience) has had the most meaning for you, and why.

Playing lacrosse in the spring of my Sophomore year gave me a new perspective about people and the stereotypes we place on them. Before playing lacrosse, I had always categorized those who lived only for sports as being too "one-sided", and I valued more highly those people whose interests were more diverse. After playing lacrosse and discovering I was not very good at it, I learned to respect my teammates who stood out on the lacrosse field and not necessarily in the classroom. I am not strongly committed to lacrosse, but this experience helped me to change certain values and taught me to look deeper into people before I judge.

2000-2001   **Ronald Beck**   123-45-6789   APP-3

Personal Statement

This personal statement helps us become acquainted with you as an individual in ways different from courses, grades, test scores, and other objective data. Please write an essay (250-500 words) on a topic of your choice or on one of the options listed below. You may attach your essay on separate sheets (same size, please). Also, please indicate your topic by checking the appropriate box below.

- ☒ 1. Evaluate a significant experience, achievement, or risk you have taken and its impact on you.
- ☐ 2. Discuss some issue of personal, local, national, or international concern and its importance to you.
- ☐ 3. Indicate a person who has had a significant influence on you, and describe that influence.
- ☐ 4. Describe a character in fiction, a historical figure, or a creative work (as in art, music, science, etc.) that has had an influence on you, and explain that influence.
- ☐ 5. Topic of your choice.

I understand that: (1) it is my responsibility to report any changes in my schedule to the colleges to which I am applying, and (2) if I am an Early Action or Early Decision Candidate, that I must attach a letter with this application notifying that college of my intent.

My signature below indicates that all information in my application is complete, factually correct, and honestly presented.

Signature *Ronald Beck*   Date *10/14/00*

These colleges are committed to administer all educational policies and activities without discrimination on the basis of race, color, religion, national or ethnic origin, age, handicap, or sex. The admissions process at private undergraduate institutions is exempt from the federal regulation implementing Title IX of the Education Amendments of 1972.

2000-2001   Ronald Beck   123-45-6789   APP-4

PERSONAL ESSAY

QUESTION

Evaluate a significant experience, achievement, or risk that you have taken and it's impact on you.

ANSWER

Let me set the scene: close to one hundred people are crammed into the small dojo with mirrored walls. The observers are there to witness their friends and family be tested on the most advanced and difficult karate forms before they can receive their black belts. My father and I are two of the six candidates (I am sixteen at the time.) We have been regularly attending Tae Kwon Do classes, at least once a week, for over five years. In an effort to convince myself that I really know what I'm doing, I reflect back on the early days when I was just a little kid taking a beginner's course in Tae Kwon Do with my dad "just for kicks" (pun definitely intended.)

White Belt: I am ten years old. My mother and sister get this brilliant idea that they want to take Tae Kwon Do to learn self-defense. Having nothing better to do, I decide to join them. Two weeks later, with sore muscles and dragging spirits, my mom and sister decide they're not ready to make a commitment. But, I am. My dad, remembering how much fun he had as my scout leader, decides that Tae Kwon Do lessons with me would be another experience he would like to share. We go once a week, usually on Sunday, and have lots of fun.

Yellow Belt: Things start to get more complicated. Not only are the Tae Kwon Do moves more intricate, but we're both discovering how hard it is to get up early on a dark, wintry Sunday morning. Dad and I definitely have to work harder at Tae Kwon Do and getting out of bed. We realize we have a problem, so we have a man-to-man talk. "Are we going to do this or aren't we?" We discuss how little time we have during the week to be with each other. We ponder whether taking Tae Kwon Do is a good use of our time. We come to the conclusion: we want to prove that we are men of our word who will stand by a commitment, and we want to do this together.

Green Belt: I am now eleven years old, and I have entered junior high school. This is a tough transition. I'm meeting for the first time all the kids who attended the other elementary schools in my town. I am not yet sure who my friends are. Some kids try to make fun of my commitment to Tae Kwon Do. They say, "That's for five year olds." I don't remember what I say to them, but I do know that even if I felt embarrassed, I was not willing to give in to them. Dad and I continue our weekly lessons, and deep down I feel proud of myself.

Purple Belt: I don't know how he does it. My dad crams down a whole bagel smothered with cream cheese; watching him makes me sick. Today is a test day; my dad and I are Purple Belts and we're going for our Red belts. I am so nervous I can't even eat the bagel dad got for me for breakfast. This test is going to be much harder than all the others. The new forms we have learned are much harder to memorize and also much longer. I hate taking these tests. We have to perform our forms in front of everyone, and if we screw up, everyone knows. It's my turn. I'm up in front of Grand Master, and my face is red with embarrassment. I bow tentatively and wait in the ready position. My body remembers the moves and carries me through the test. Dad and I become Red Belts.

Red Belt: I have finally reached the point where the "fun and games" are over and the study of Tae Kwon Do becomes more serious. Fortunately, I have discovered a hidden benefit of Tae Kwon Do: it offers a therapeutic way to release my stress. As a Red Belt, I am now allowed to break wood, which shows me how I could channel my adolescent anger productively. Unlike some of my school friends, I vent my anger at the dojo rather than at school.

Brown Belt: Dad and I prepare for our brown belt and recognize that our commitment to each other and our focus and self-discipline have been essential ingredients to accomplishing our goals. I note with pleasure that although I am one of the smallest in my class, I can hold my own when I spar against adults two or three times my size, my dad included. I am amazed that I am not intimidated by them.

As a Brown Belt, I am only one step away from becoming a Black Belt. This one step, however, requires me to remember and perform all the forms that I have learned over the past five years. Reviewing them does wonders for my self-esteem since I see how far I have come. The Brown Belt forms require speed, precision, agility, and a good memory since the forms can take five or more minutes to complete. The easier White and Yellow belt forms must be executed with perfection because they are simpler than the others, and the result is that the student is held to a much higher standard.

Dad and I review and practice our steps together. We are each others' support group and cheering squad. When we take our test for the Black Belt, we are ready, and we pass! We make a great team.

Black Belt: I am now a Black Belt and proud of it. Not only have I reached an important level of mastery, but I can defend myself in any situation. I am grateful for my experience and want to "give back" to my community some of what I have learned. I become a Tae Kwon Do instructor, and I teach both children and adults. I love it when my students call me "sir." I feel pleasure as I watch them progress. But, more importantly, with each step they take, I am reminded of how far I have come.

NOTES

NOTES

NOTES

NOTES

NOTES

NOTES